GOSPEL, CHURCH, MISSION

KENT S. KNUTSON
1924 - 1973

AUGSBURG PUBLISHING HOUSE
Minneapolis, Minnesota

GOSPEL, CHURCH, MISSION

Library of Congress Catalog Card No. 75-40632

International Standard Book No. 0-8066-1522-2

MANUFACTURED IN THE UNITED STATES OF AMERICA

Contents

Foreword

I greet you in the name of our Lord Jesus Christ. May his power, his patience, and his abundant hope stir you and shape you to his service!

Kent S. Knutson

There are times when just the right person with just the right gifts and leadership ability comes to the fore when people must choose a leader. We think of Moses and David as leaders of Israel. We remember the elections of Washington and Lincoln at crucial periods in our nation's history. Members of The American Lutheran Church were confident that Fredrik Schiotz was just the right man to bring them together when he became the church's first general president. When the mantle of leadership was to pass from Dr. Schiotz to a new president—a young systematic theologian and seminary president appeared on the scene like a meteor in the sky, displaying those gifts and style of leadership which matched the challenges and needs of the hour.

Kent Knutson seemed to be just the right man for the right time of The American Lutheran Church. But Kent Knutson and all that he was didn't just happen. As the biography shows, Kent became what he was for our time by God's grace, through careful and loving nurture at home, and by disciplined and dedicated application of himself to the study of theology. He also had a strong and sensitive pastoral heart. His church was naturally led to choose him not only to teach theology but also to serve as the head of one of its theological seminaries. Like a magnificent rose his life blossomed from its roots, through years of growth and training into that moment when he became the president of The American Lutheran Church.

In this volume we intend to bring together the significant elements of Kent Knutson's life and then allow him to speak again through printed selections from his lectures, speeches, and writings. In the biography by E. Clifford Nelson, who was one of Kent's theological colleagues and a constant friend throughout his career, we gain a moving insight into the factors of home, education, family and church which converged into the life of Kent Knutson.

The major portion of the book is a selection from a collection of Kent Knutson's statements and writings. We are indebted to the careful work of Professors Frank Benz, Ralph Quere, and William Streng for the selection of material.

In making the selection the guiding principle was followed that material already published in one or the other of the books, *God's Drama in Seven Acts, His Only Son Our Lord,* and the *Shape of the Question,* would not be included.

First is a collection of clear, crisp, brilliant statements for which Knutson was so well known. The statements which have been chosen are those that were so clear in themselves that they would not be distorted by being printed in isolation from their context or by being arranged alphabetically! This material is arranged in three sections: 1) Gospel; 2) Church; 3) Mission.

Then there follows a selection of longer quotations and a few complete articles giving a more complete development of a number of theological and pastoral issues. Here the reader can follow the careful way a theologian looks at all sides of a statement about God, Christ, the Church, in order to make more clear the unqualified grace by which God has related to man in Christ. These longer excerpts were selected to correspond with many of the same questions which are of vital concern to the church today. Dr. Knutson's insights on such issues can be helpful to the whole church in its life today and tomorrow. The reader will find not only many quotations that are remembered with nostalgia from a speech or an article in *The Lutheran Standard,* but even more the reader will find expressions about the gospel, the church, and its mission which are extremely helpful as we seek to know who we are as God's people and how God's people do the gospel. The several longer features, comprising either an entire address or a major section of a speech, letter, or statement, give us a brief in-depth treatment of certain teachings of the church (e.g. baptism), though he himself would not have regarded any of these as finished formulations. These longer articles are listed in chronological order.

This book has been a joint effort of Augsburg Publishing House and Wartburg Theological Seminary and is sent forth to all the pastors of The American Lutheran Church. As by God's grace Kent Knutson stepped with buoyant and firm step into the life and leadership of The American Lutheran Church, it is our hope that the biography and selection of his writings will help and inspire us all to carry on that concept of ministry to which he was committed. Perhaps Kent Knutson's concept of ministry is best illustrated by one of his statements at the conclusion of his evangelism address at the 1972 convention of The ALC. There he declared: "Obey Him! Obey Him! And then you may hope, then you may celebrate, and then your destiny becomes alive, for Jesus Christ is your Savior and your Lord, and your friend." As one of the pastors of the church said about this summary of Kent Knutson's life and ministry, "this one sentence summarizes the message he has for us as we continue where he left off."

The faculties and staffs of Luther and Wartburg seminaries were pleased to have the honor of helping to edit this book as a testimony to God's grace in the life of Kent Knutson. We want to express special thanks to Norma Knutson and children, Kirsten, Kris, Kent, Kaia, Kimberly, and Karl, and to Anne (Mrs. Charles Kanten), Milderd (Mrs. Harold Knutson), and Gerhard Knutson. They have helped us all to comprehend anew what it means to celebrate the victory of God's grace in the resurrection of our Lord Jesus Christ.

WILLIAM H. WEIBLEN

Kent Sigvart Knutson
1924-1973
A Biographical Sketch

Some day a definitive biography of Kent Sigvart Knutson may be written. What follows is a vignette which is impressionistic and subjective. It is to be hoped none the less that it can be a faithful picture of a "grace-full" man.

We have lived close enough to him to observe his style of life, to sense some of his God-given abilities and to experience his child-like faith. This personal proximity has likewise served to detect and thus to prevent the growth and accretion of legends about an ecclesiastical hero. We know only too well the myth-making ability of a community and, although there may be some basis in fact for the myths and the legends, this propensity must not be allowed to dominate or even color our evaluation of a genuinely great churchman.

Therefore, the purpose of this statement is to paint a portrait of a quiet friend, a diligent workman, a loyal colleague, and a vigorous leader who stood among us as a gift from God. There may not be many "warts" on the portrait, but there will be evidence that our admiration is always tempered by the fact that Kent Knutson was a genuine human being, subject to all the temptations to which the flesh is heir.

The basic purpose, then, is introductory rather than biographical. That is, our chronicle will seek to lead the reader into a sympathetic understanding of the selected writings that form the major part of this book. The biographical background is important but secondary. It is very important because it will point out some of the historical circumstances that were the context out of which Kent Knutson spoke and wrote. It is secondary because the primary purpose of the book is to let the man speak for himself. Therefore, one cannot stress over much that this is a biographical *sketch,* an outline that requires later fleshing out; an impressionistic interpretation by an older colleague who watched with joy and sometimes with sheer amazement the disciplined development of a devoted family man, a pious theologian, and a visionary (I do not use the word pejoratively) ecclesiastical leader.

The selection of works from his pen has been guided by the hope that the heart and mind of their author will not only be preserved as a historical artifact for posterity but as an earnest call to Christians everywhere to find inspiration in evangelical fidelity, broad-gauged churchmanship, missionary enthusiasm, and magnificent hopes for this world and the next.

The substance of the story could quite justifiably be summarized in the simple word "grace." But Kent Knutson would ask, as he did in his final public address, what is grace? Is it "Amazing Grace"? Yes, he would answer, but he knew that other religions included among their tenets a doctrine of grace. So, he said, we must be more specific; we must speak of "the grace of God manifested in Christ Jesus." This is what Article IV of the Augsburg Confession proclaimed: Justification "by grace, for Christ's sake, through faith." (Theodore Tappert, ed., *Book of Concord,* p. 30.) Knutson was a Lutheran!

The Chronicle

Lake Lutheran Church, (Renwick, Iowa, 4 miles south, 1½ miles west) situated in the fertile countryside of north central Iowa, has an odd name, at least to a stranger. There is no lake within miles; just good black earth that at today's prices, sells as high as $1400.00 an acre. It is a typical small white frame church with a truncated tower, the steeple having been toppled no doubt by an Iowa summer storm. The chancel is like hundreds of others in rural mid-America where so many Lutherans live. The font is at the left, the pulpit at the right, the altar and communion rail at the center. In these simple surroundings Kent Knutson's life in God began and was nurtured. As far as Lake Lutheran Church was concerned, Kent Knutson's pilgrimage went full circle: from baptism to burial. It was here on a raw blustery day in March, 1973, that the funeral service for a son of the congregation was held. He was interred under a spruce tree in the church yard where names like Gangstead, Harvey, Luthro, and Oppedahl marked other gravesites. Taken from the surrounding soil, a rough field stone chiseled by the St. Olaf College sculptor Arnold Flaten will bear these symbols: Kent Sigvart Knutson, 1924-1973, and a cross. A name, a life, and the cross.

The last book written by Kent Knutson was a modest piece entitled *The Shape of the Question* (Minneapolis: Augsburg, 1972) and dealt with a persisting theme: the nature of the church, its ministry and mission in this secular age. In the Preface he speaks a caveat: "This big question cannot be answered in one book. But its shape can be examined."

Something analogous must be said about our attempts to chronicle and assess his short but far-reaching life. If *he* found it necessary to say of his book that it really could not address "the big question" but had to limit itself to the "shape" of the question, we find ourselves in a similar predicament. We can only examine the "shape," the contours of a life that continues to influence Christians throughout the world.

Although this limitation is one of the "givens" in this undertaking, it must be stated that "the shape" or the contours of any life have their sharp points. We might call them "turning-points," or better, decisive moments that provide hints to the understanding of a career in the making. Among these, in Knutson's case, were his family background and experiences, his student days, his military service, his short-lived career as a chemical engineer, his wife and children, his decisions and goals as pastor, theological professor, seminary president, and finally as the pastor of pastors and ecumenical leader in The American Lutheran Church.

I

By most American standards Knutson was born into modest, if not humble, surroundings. His father, Gunner Knutson Gilje (pronounced Yilye) was born in western Norway on the North Sea. The farm Gilje was located on a fresh water lake connected to the sea by a narrow channel by which Gunner's father and other commercial fishermen could reach the coastal fishing grounds and thus supplement their meager incomes from the tiny and rocky farms that dotted the countryside. Gunner knew that when he was confirmed (at 14 years of age) he would have to seek his own fortune, for by the ancient custom of primogeniture the farm would descend to the oldest son. Gunner, a sturdy, dark-haired lad, square-jawed, short, and stocky, did what thousands of his young countrymen were doing. He went "down to the sea in ships." Vessels of the Norwegian merchant marine carried him to many of the world's important ports. He saw New York and New Orleans, Hong Kong and Singapore, the coastal cities of South America and Africa.

But in time he had enough of the seaman's life. He had a longing to settle somewhere on the American west coast, perhaps in San Francisco, a city he had seen after its rapid rebuilding following the devastating earthquake in 1906. With this in mind, he left his ship in New York and found his way to Iowa to visit a relative, Jacob Gunderson. The fertile Iowa farms looked good to the young man who remembered the thin-soiled and rocky plots of his homeland. It took little argument to persuade him to consider what today is called agribusiness. The black Iowa soil, fertile though it might be, was flat and without drainage. The spring thaws and rainy seasons left the land virtually unworkable. Hence it needed to be tiled. The enterprising young immigrant found a partner and the two men built a tile factory in Goldfield, Iowa, where they soon established a thriving business. In fact, the promise of prosperity led Gunner back to Norway to the girl who was still waiting for him. Six years younger than he, Gertrude Thorsheim was the daughter of the local school teacher. In the stratified society of Norway the caste system persisted into the twentieth century. This meant that it was hardly fitting for the daughter of the local intellectual to marry the son of a fisherman-farmer. But love conquered all and Gunner and Gertrude were married in 1921. By March of that year the bridegroom had brought his bride across the rough North Atlantic to Iowa's muddy springtime fields; it was a depressing sight for one accustomed to the rugged beauty of western Norway. But the initial loneliness and homesickness gradually disappeared. Gunner prospered and purchased a fine home. Here Kent Sigvart Knutson was born, August 7, 1924.

In due course, three other children joined the family: Anne (now Mrs. Charles Kanten, Milan, Minnesota), Gerhard (Minneapolis, Minnesota), and Mildred (Mrs. Harold Knutson, Eagle Grove, Iowa). Kent was not only the first-born, but the natural leader, and one who quickly became his father's alter-ego. In many respects Kent took on a "father image" to the rest of the family. Mildred reported that "Pop" (as they all called him) was 49 years old when she was born and that she turned naturally to her older brother, Bud (Kent's nickname in the family), for paternal care. As an adult she once complained to Bud that she could not remember having sat on Pop's lap. To this Bud answered, "But remember all the times you sat on my lap." Even Pop, who was a community leader, came in time to depend on Kent. On one occasion, the family recalled, Pop was informed that he had a lip cancer that needed immediate attention. At the time Kent was no longer at home, having long since set out on his own career. Pop refused to go to the hospital. When asked "Why?" he answered, "I want to talk to Bud first."

So Kent was a leader in the family. Sometimes, however, this talent for leadership was unkindly applied. On one occasion Pop had taken the children to the county fair where the number on Mildred's ticket gave her the right to choose a bicycle from a row of shiny prizes. Kent took charge and insisted that a boy's bicycle was much more desirable and practical than a girl's bicycle. Mildred complained later: "When I finally learned how to ride it, Kent took it off to college with him!"

On a later occasion the family decided that Mom and Pop should visit their homeland. The two girls and the two boys would run the farm in their absence. Although college-educated Kent had largely lost his interest in farming, he soon organized the management of the farm by assigning duties to each. Everything ran smoothly until one day twelve year old Mildred, in a rebellious mood, refused to do her chores of gathering the eggs and corn cobs. Kent picked her up by the arms, carried her out doors, and lectured her all the way to the barn on the Fourth Commandment! Naturally Mildred was not happy about this high-handed manner, although she admitted later that, despite his being a firm, "no-nonsense boss," he was never mean. His authority was always tempered with love.

Gerhard and the two sisters actually knew much more about the farm and possessed an expertise that Kent had lost. But Kent utilized their strengths in such a manner that, when the parents returned, the farm had realized a sizable profit. "But we must admit," said Gerhard and Mildred, "that while we did the work, Kent and Anne spent an unconscionable amount of time in the front room discussing philosophy, politics and religion."

Kent was also a leader in school, and this pattern continued when he went off to college. He would like to have attended St. Olaf College, but the Depression and his father's assumption that St. Olaf was primarily a "minister's school" dictated a decision to attend a state school. Iowa State College at nearby Ames, therefore, seemed the best choice. His major academic pursuits, at least at the beginning, were in the field of science. Despite the need to work his way through collge, he was to graduate with honors in chemical engineering. But his interests and leadership were not limited to his area of special competence. He was on the editorial staff of the student paper for the School of Engineering; he developed his appreciation of music by being a member of the university band; and, perhaps most important of all, he began to probe the depths of his Lutheran heritage by activity in the campus religious organizations. He was a member of the Inter-Faith Council, the YMCA, the Religious Emphasis Week Committee, and president of the Lutheran Student Association. The attributes of his later churchmanship were already in evidence: intellectual brilliance, natural leadership, inherited and cultivated piety.

His academic career was interrupted during his senior year (1944) by military service in the United States Navy. Stationed at Corpus Christi, Texas, where he received a year of electronics training, he found himself, after the war, sitting out the boredom of the U.S.A. military presence in the Philippines. He returned to Iowa State somewhat hesitantly but quickly resumed his courses and was graduated in the early spring of 1947. In a matter of weeks he had accepted a position with Standard Oil Company in the Process Design Section of the Research Department at Whiting,

Indiana. The day after his arrival he wrote his parents in wonder and awe about Standard Oil's Whiting plant: ". . . one of the world's largest refineries [occupying] 1000 acres. . . . Standard runs the town. . . . I have a choice of 3 places (Pilot Plant, Technical Service, and Design). I chose design. . . . I think I'll enjoy it. I have 2 stenographers at my disposal (!!) who will take dictation [and] I share an office with my boss. . . . I like everything so far [except] the trains. . . . A train goes every couple minutes and shakes the whole town. . . . Love, Bud."

With high enthusiasm he plunged into his work and soon developed a design for what was called a "batch fractionator" to produce naphtha gas. The Knutson device, which is still in operation, was housed in a large tower where derivatives of petroleum were "picked off" at critical temperatures. In later years, after he left Standard Oil, Knutson could check on "his invention" visually as he drove through Hammond, Indiana, where the fractionator was located.

Although he enjoyed his work and gave himself to it unstintingly, he came to the conviction that a career in scientific research could not provide him with satisfying goals and a sense of fulfillment. Ever since his confirmation in Lake Lutheran Church the thought of service in the ordained ministry occupied the back of his mind. He had always been a serious individual, so serious, in fact, that friends wondered if he ever had any "fun." Did he have any hobbies beyond his books and work? Could he break away from the task at hand to enjoy leisure?

"Yes," answered his sister Anne. "We used to have lots of fun together. I recall when he was at Whiting and I was a sophomore at St. Olaf College, Kent wanted me to see what the big city was like. So I got a summer job (1947) at the Lutheran Deaconess Hospital in Chicago, and every weekend Kent showed me the city. We had fun! We did things I never dreamed of. We went to symphony concerts in Grant Park and Ravinia. We saw stage plays, baseball games, the Ringling Brothers Circus, and the museums. Kent was fascinated by the dynamics of the city. He loved the city whether it was Chicago, New York, Paris, or Rome. The city got into his blood. I wonder if his later concerns for relating the gospel to the secular world was not rooted in his belief that the city shaped the mind and mood of modern America. And in the midst of all this he kept advising me how best to use my college years, what books to read, how to interpret political and social events. My very big brother had fun but he always returned to the serious questions of living our lives meaningfully in this secular age."

II

The serious and reflective young scientist found himself questioning what he was doing in Whiting. Standard Oil of Indiana had provided him with what most young men would have described as a golden opportunity plus a grand salary. Wasn't $5000.00 grand for a young man just out of college, and doubly grand when compared to what others were being paid in 1947? And the possibilities of advancement? Surely they were rosy and alluring. Yet despite all this Kent Knutson worked at his projects with a sense of unease. The more he thought about it, the more distressed he became. As a chemical engineer he was but a cog in a big machine. He had mastered the basics of chemistry; he knew the formulae and the equations. His superiors challenged him with projects and problems. These were to be met by simply applying scientific knowledge and skills. Moreover, all of this could be done in solitude with pencil, paper, and knowledge of chemistry. It seemed so impersonal and detached from life. Of course, he had no way of knowing that by the mid-1970s a world energy crisis might transform his scientific detachment into something intensely personal and even redemptive in a secular sense. But in 1947 he was a lonely scientist yearning for the kind of personal involvement that he had experienced as a worker and leader in student religious conferences, not least the enriching fellowship with colleagues in the Lutheran Students Association. From leaders in the Lutheran campus ministry, such as Alvin Rogness, Fredrik Schiotz, and Joseph L. Knutson, he had been introduced to a world of ultimate concerns.

Now, acting especially on the counsel of Alvin Rogness, he inquired whether a scientifically educated college graduate, could qualify for admission to a theological seminary. He had a profound sense of academic inadequacy, especially in the field of liberal arts. When some encouragement was given, he made a trip to his home in Iowa to discuss the problem with his family. His younger brother recalls that he and Kent walked through the cornfields, pulling out cockleburrs and talking about his spiritual struggle. Rogness, who had served Lutheran students while pastor at Ames and was now at nearby Mason City, meanwhile pleaded his cause with the president of the seminary, and the decision was virtually made to begin theological study. His parents received the news with both pleasure and puzzlement. Mom Knutson expressed her feelings by tears of happiness. Pop had some difficulty. Why would somebody with such a good position now want to give it up for the prosaic job of a minister? But, he said, "If this is what you really want to do, then you must do it."

Shortly before the seminary opened its doors for the autumn term in 1947, Kent left his office at Standard Oil, boarded a train for St. Paul, Minnesota, and arrived the night before registration began. Most of the new students were graduates of church-related colleges and had some of the traditional preparation for the study of theology. The chemical engineer felt ill at ease in the new environment, but conscious of the lacunae in his education, he set himself with determination to the twofold task of filling in the lacks and immersing himself in theological studies.

During the next four years, he supplemented the seminary curriculum with courses in philosophy and history at the nearby University of Minnesota, especially during his internship (1949-1950) with the Twin City Lutheran Student Foundation where he worked in association with the Rev. William Larsen, the Lutheran campus pastor. His interest in continuing and broadening his educational base and maintaining close ties with the academic world were enhanced by the opportunity to attend the International Summer School of the University of Oslo in 1949, and his election to a high position in the Lutheran Student Association in America. During his senior year (1950-1951) he served as national president of the LSAA. To nobody's surprise he conducted his office with great skill and efficiency, traveled from coast to coast to keep in touch with regional and local LSAs and cultivated a burgeoning interest in the ecumenical movement as espoused by the United Student Christian Council (USCC). In these ways the chemical engineer was rapidly becoming a young churchman with national and international contacts.

But this was not all. The Lutheran Student Movement (incidentally, he seems to have coined this name which was officially adopted in 1969) introduced him to a young lady, Norma Elizabeth Arnesen of Brooklyn, New York. Norma, a graduate of St. Olaf College, was Western Regional Director for the Division of College and University Work of the National Lutheran Council with offices in Chicago, where she worked in close association with the new executive secretary, Donald R. Heiges, one of Kent's friends in the campus ministry. Norma's duties brought her into the orbit of Kent's acquaintances, some of whom were women counselors for

Lutheran university students and as such were directly responsible to Norma. Let Norma tell the story:

"No, I didn't know Kent then, but I knew a great deal about him from these counselors. That summer (1950) the LSAA Ashram and National Council met at Blue Ridge, North Carolina. Kent was a member of the council which later elected him national president. I can remember when I arrived at Blue Ridge I was wearing a yellow suit and felt pretty dressed up, coming to a summer camp. In any case, a fellow came out to help me with my suitcases, and oh, was he a mess! He had a pen in his sweatshirt and it had leaked all over it. He had ink on the side of his face. He looked just awful. I asked him his name and he said, 'Kent Knutson.' I blurted out, 'You're Kent Knutson!' I looked at him with curiosity. Was this the fellow my counselors had been talking about?"

"When were we married? About a year later. You see, as national president of the LSAA, Kent turned up at meetings all over the country, meetings that I also attended. At first we were just sort of friends. But soon he wrote his sister Anne, 'I'm in love and her name is Norma Arnesen. I can't study, I can't eat. I'm in love!' The night we became engaged we were walking along the Lake Shore Drive in Chicago. An April rain drenched us. There in the downpour he asked me to marry him. When I said yes, I wasn't quite sure. The next morning when we met, I asked him, 'Did you sleep?' He said, 'No, I wondered all night if I'd made a mistake.'"

It was not a mistake and on September 15, 1951 they were married at Trinity Church, Brooklyn, where Norma's parents, Colonel and Mrs. S. J. Arnesen were members. Norma's father was the publisher of a Norwegian language newspaper, *Nordisk Tidende*. Her mother, a gentle soul of refined tastes, was of Danish extraction. So Norma and Kent's first children (Kirsten, Kristofer, Kent, and Kaia) were Scandinavians; the last two were Korean (Kimberly and Karl). But more about that later.

III

Before Knutson had graduated from the seminary, he had written about his plans for the future. He reported: "During my internship I saw the urgent need for student pastors with advanced degrees, pastors who would have the respect and confidence of the university officials and faculty. I have consequently made application to the graduate schools of Union Theological Seminary and Columbia University to plan to begin work there. . . . When I have obtained my doctorate and after experience as a parish pastor, I hope to be called to work with college students in some capacity." It should be added here that Kent was also haunted by a sense of personal educational inadequacy, and his entrance upon graduate work was evidence of his eagerness to fill in the gaps.

With this program before them, Kent and Norma set up housekeeping in a small Manhattan apartment. While Kent pursued his graduate studies, Norma re-entered the employ of the National Lutheran Council, not in the campus ministry, but as editor of the council's official organ, *The National Lutheran*. School and living expenses were paid from G.I. Bill income, and Norma's salary went into the bank with the hope that they might spend the next year in Europe.

Meanwhile, Kent organized life in the Manhattan apartment. There was to be no housecleaning or laundry on weekends. These days were to be free for seeing the city and attending church. But with both partners at work, this schedule required expert planning. Norma described it: "Kent knew how to organize things. He organized that little apartment and he even organized me. Then we would wander down Fifth Avenue and Broadway, looking at shops, and buildings, and people. That's what Kent wanted to do. Then there were little off-Broadway movie houses. Kent loved movies, and every movie was a theological experience. Outside the movie house he would start explaining the theological meaning of the movie maker's art. He'd collect an audience and tell anyone who would listen that these movies were comments on our society and the meaning of life. I'd be so embarrassed, but he just got excited by all these meanings that he saw in the cinematic symbols."

The year sped by and in June, 1952, the young couple was off for Europe. June was spent in Norway visiting relatives. July was spent in Germany where American friends helped them with some temporary living quarters, arranged for a tutor in German, a Frau Mueller-Freienfeld, and introduced Kent to members of the theological faculty at Heidelberg where he planned to spend the academic year 1952-1953. Among the summer experiences were attendance at the Second Assembly of the Lutheran World Federation, Hannover, where Kent and Norma were official visitors from the Evangelical Lutheran Church. Moreover, he participated as a student delegate in the Third World Conference on Faith and Order, Lund, Sweden. These assemblies made deep impressions on both Kent and Norma.

Kent was especially fascinated by the theological debate at Lund. He had been toying with the idea of writing his doctoral dissertation on the doctrine of the church in the ecumenical movement. As early as his presidency of the Lutheran Student Association of America his reports indicated a growing preoccupation with the doctrine of the church and its mission. The ecumenical discussion of the ecclesiological question at Lund in 1952 took a sharp turn away from earlier studies in comparative ecclesiology. Swedish theologian, Anders Nygren, pointed out that these discussions could only lead into a cul de sac and that if there was to be growth in an ecumenical understanding of the church, one must begin at the center, namely with Jesus Christ. This seemingly obvious and simple observation was nevertheless the crux of the problem and henceforth Faith and Order turned its theological attention to a

Christological interpretation of ecclesiology. This was not lost on Kent Knutson, and later at the University of Heidelberg, especially under the tutelage of Professor Edmund Schlink, Kent's own theologically ecumenical churchmanship took shape.

During the year at Heidelberg he kept live contacts with acquaintances in the World Student Christian Federation (WSCF), the Lutheran World Federation, and Faith and Order of the World Council of Churches. Before they returned to America, however, they suffered a great sorrow. Their first child, Kirsten, died shortly after birth and was buried in Heidelberg. Their second child, born after they had resumed life in America, was also to be named Kirsten, now Mrs. Donald Patterson.

The years 1953-1958 were spent in Brooklyn and Staten Island, New York. Upon their return from Heidelberg they lived in a Brooklyn apartment near Norma's relatives. Kent, meanwhile, resumed his doctoral work, and after what Norma called "feverish preparation," he took his qualifying examinations for the Ph.D. With this done, he began in February, 1954, to concentrate on the writing of a dissertation in the general area of Faith and Order. Conditionally accepted by the faculty committee, his topic needed the final approval of his "doctor father," Professor Wilhelm Pauck who was on leave of absence. Meanwhile, Kent read thoroughly, outlined the project, but, then to his dismay, received word from Pauck that the topic was not acceptable. This blow came shortly after he had accepted a call to become pastor of Our Saviour Lutheran Church, Staten Island, and just before he and the family (Kirsten had been born in October, 1953) were to leave for Iowa where he was to be ordained by Alvin Rogness in his home congregation, Lake Lutheran Church, on May 30, 1954.

Life on Staten Island was exciting and strenuous. In fact, in retrospect the work looked like something from Rabelais: it was gargantuan. First, of course, was the task of learning to know the congregation, of preparing sermons and of pastoring a people. Secondly, there was the challenge of erecting a superstructure on the basement church (which Kent described as big enough to be "the foundation for a young cathedral"). Thirdly, there was the unfinished doctoral dissertation. Having agreed with Professor Pauck that contemporary Lutherans needed a fresh look at Luther's understanding of the doctrine of the church, he finally settled on an acceptable topic: "The Community of Faith and the World: An Inquiry into the Concept of the Church in Contemporary Lutheranism."

Only those who have experienced it will know what researching and writing a doctoral dissertation in Kent's situation was like. After all, the congregation must always be given the priority, and in Kent's case it was. The building of the church came next, and the dissertation received bits and pieces of time between 1954 and 1961 when the degree was finally won.

Meanwhile, the family grew. Kristopher was born in June, 1955; and young Kent, in November 1956. During the summer of 1957 both Kent and Norma were asked by the Director of the Lutheran World Assembly (to be held in Minneapolis) to edit the Assembly's eight page daily newspaper. Norma had attended both previous assemblies (Lund, 1947, and Hannover, 1952), and as noted, Kent had been at Hannover. Editing the Assembly paper proved to be an almost superhuman venture. It was undertaken with an undersized staff and budget, but, as had been expected, was accomplished with a brilliance that caught the magnificence of the event in accurate reporting and insightful interpretation.

The following year, in March, 1958, Kent received a call to become an assistant professor at his alma mater, Luther Theological Seminary in St. Paul. He was to teach in the department of systematic theology with the tacit understanding that time would be provided for the completion of his dissertation. Actually it was this unwritten codicil that softened the pain of departure from Staten Island where roots had sunk deep into the life of the parish. Our Saviour Church was a vital congregation. Moreover, the new church was being built, the finances were in good order, and growth was healthy. In his letter of resignation, the pastor said: "For me, the call to the seminary certainly involves more work and responsibility than continuing as pastor here. And it means the sadness of leaving just at the moment when many of the fruits of our labor together are reaching their climax." By mid-summer the Knutson family was on its way to the metropolitan center of the upper midwest, and, from one point of view (that of church population), the capital of American Lutheranism.

IV

It was a new life. The urban congregation with its hectic round of duties was left behind. Committee meetings, council meetings, building meetings, teachers' meetings, meetings, meetings, and more meetings, the seemingly necessary bane of all parish pastors who in most cases longed for more time to prepare sermons, to teach both children and adults, and to make pastoral visits on the sick and the well, and to direct community evangelism, was now history. However, the new faculty member quickly discovered that the seminary was not an ivory tower. In fact, once again "meetings," though different in nature and purpose, intruded themselves on the dissertation and a father's care for a growing family. A fourth child, Kaia, was born in February, 1960; and later (after the Knutsons moved to Wartburg Seminary, Dubuque, Iowa), two native Korean children (Kimberly, born in 1960, and Karl, born in 1964) were received into the warmth and love of the Knutson family.

With customary dedication and energy Kent approached life in the academic world. Although he had never been a professional teacher, he soon made it evident that the faculty had acquired a brilliant classroom leader. Many were the students who reported to the president and this writer (who was Dean of the Faculty during several of Kent's years at Luther Seminary) that this teacher of systematic theology was nothing if not systematic. But more than that, he was Socratic, provocative, always prodding the student to give a reason for the hope that was in him. But he was a pastor, too. Systematic theology was his love, but he had a greater love, the personal knowledge of the grace of God in Christ, the dynamic presence of the Triune God in creation, redemption, and salvation of mankind, and the conviction that the church must be the church in this secular world.

The Knutson family Christmas letter in 1961 reported: "This has been the year of the post-doctorate [the degree was awarded that year]. At first we gloried in the new freedom—then Kent was made the Director of Graduate School at the Seminary and became involved in the production of a new theological journal, *Dialog,* which makes its debut in January [1962]."

It was especially his contributions to this journal and his editorship of the Tower Books (Augsburg Publishing House) that identified Kent Knutson as a leading figure in a rising generation of young Lutheran scholars and theologians in the United States. Although deeply committed to an evangelical and ecumenical Lutheran confessionality, these men were often judged as critics of the church. Their journal was seen as the mouthpiece for "young Turks" who were little more than propagandists for avant-gardist theological, political, and social views. How history will treat these men and what they stood for is yet to be seen. In any case, though solidly aligned with the "neo-Lutheranism" of *Dialog,* Knutson was a careful, responsible, and loving critic of the church. He invariably won the confidence of his students and colleagues, and, in a remarkably short time, of the church at large, both in America and abroad. Often a lecturer at theological conferences and "lay schools," and a frequent contributor to a growing circle of publications whose editors saw in him a seminal figure, Kent had established himself as a vigorous spokesman for Lutheran unity, ecumenical responsibility, social and political awareness, and, not least, the immense role of theological education in the life of the church.

It was not strange, therefore, that when the presidency of Wartburg Theological Seminary became vacant, his name was on the list of nominees to fill the post. Kent had long discussions over the telephone and around the kitchen table of close friends about his future service to the church. Would his voice be more effective in the classroom of a large seminary in St. Paul or would it be given more attention in policy-making ecclesiastical circles as president of Wartburg Seminary? He finally decided that, should the church choose him to become Wartburg's leader, he would subordinate his deep love for the classroom for the president's desk. As we have noted, this decision did not come lightly. Moreover, despite the impression of mastery, Kent agonized over his inadequacies, an agony that led him increasingly to place himself in God's gracious hands. He had been granted a leave of absence in 1963-1964 to write a layman's text in Christology and to read in the field of theology and philosophy, especially in the area of linguistic analysis. This, of course, was all done to better equip himself as a teacher of pastors, and placed him under obligation to a theological school which he dearly loved. This but added to his inner turmoil.

But when the American Lutheran Church, meeting in convention at Omaha in 1968, elected him to the presidency of Wartburg, the die was cast, and on January 1, 1969, he began his new duties in Dubuque. Catapulted into positions of responsible leadership he rapidly matured in his role as administrator.

To understand how he saw his new role it is helpful to quote excerpts from his acceptance speech in Omaha on October 19, 1968. After referring to his early decision to move from his position with Standard Oil into the ministry of the church, he continued:

> I consider the gravity of my decision [today] to be as great as that vocational decision 21 years ago. . . . The task you have given me is not easy. . . . . I consider your call to me to be not only administrative but more primarily to engage in a struggle with three basic questions. First, what is theological education? A seminary once had the image of a sleepy place . . . but three new elements are now with us [Knutson then elaborated briefly on the new and lively student generation, the explosion of theological knowledge, and the ecumenical context of theological education]. But this question cannot be answered without examining [a second] question, What is the ministry? . . . The new pastor [today] must be skilled in pastoral work, in the dynamics of social concerns, in organizational prowess, in the handling of his own emotional stress [all of which is] in addition to sound theological competence. . . . We must decide for what we are training a man. But again, there is a more fundamental question facing us. . . . We haven't faced the crisis which underlies everything we do —the crisis of the identity of the church: What is the church? We know how to define the church theologically. . . . But we do not know how to translate this definition into our life in the world. . . . These [three] questions will be a continuing part of the responsibilities of the call you have given me.

Knutson continued by pledging himself to the "empowering force of the gospel," and the Lutheran confessions as "the most cogent witness to that gospel in Christendom." And, finally, he asked the church, some of whose members were uneasy with the new problems in theology, to pledge him its trust and cooperation. This brief talk, on which he elaborated extensively in his inaugural address on September 19, 1969, became the keynote of his administration.

The inauguration itself, according to one of the Wartburg faculty members, was a portent of the Knutson way of doing things. Recognizing that the faculty's morale was depressed by questions concerning the future of the seminary, the new president brought a spirit of hopefulness to the campus by using the occasion to call the attention of the church at large and the local community to Wartburg's past and future role in theological education. A colleague observed: "Never had so many different professors, church administrators, bishops and dignitaries visited the campus of Wartburg Seminary at one time." Heightened awareness of the more than a century old school prompted a leading local Jewish businessman to say: "Wartburg has got to be the best kept secret in Dubuque."

In assessing the significance of Knutson's short tenure at Wartburg, his friend and successor in office, Professor William Weiblen, pointed to a half-dozen areas in which Knutson bequeathed a lasting legacy to the seminary. Above all, he said, was his decisive leadership which brought courage and confidence to both faculty and students. The school became a "family" characterized by intellectual rigor, religious dedication, social cohesiveness, ecumenical outreach, secular and political sensitivities. All of these indications of close cooperation, profound affection, and firm loyalties were tested when it became known in the summer of 1970 that Kent was one of the leading candidates for the presidency of the church.

He immediately took the faculty into his confidence and asked them to counsel him. The result was that, when indeed he was elected, the faculty was both proud and sad; proud in that one of their own was singled out for such a responsibility and sad that his ministry at Wartburg was so short. A colleague said, "It was a serene Kent Knutson who went to San Antonio [the site of the church convention]. He felt at peace about the future and with himself." Although he was no doubt conscious of the strong possibility of his being elected, he neglected to pack ecclesiastical attire.

No assessment of the Wartburg years would be complete without mention of the affection with which the seminary community embraced the Knutson family as a whole. "Kent and Norma," said another colleague, "made out of their home an energy and activity center. Everything was going on all the time. Students were invited in; faculty and family and friends from all over made a steady stream of visitors. Some were invited. Many just dropped in." It was not unusual for Norma to learn in an afternoon that thirty guests would be present for evening dessert at nine o'clock.

And then there were the children. How they loved their Wartburg home and friends! And when Kimberly, the first of two Knutson Koreans, joined the family, it was not long before she shared the simple joys and the warm welcome of the Wartburg "family." When it came time for the Knutsons to leave Dubuque, Weiblen commented: "I couldn't help but notice the sadness in the eyes of the Knutson children. . . . I guess that sort of expressed where all of us were."

V

On the day of Knutson's inauguration as president of Wartburg Theological Seminary several greetings were brought at the special dinner honoring him and his family. One of these was delivered by President Donald R. Heiges of Lutheran Theological Seminary in

Gettysburg, Pennsylvania. Heiges had been asked to speak on behalf of all the Lutheran seminaries in the United States and Canada. He spoke also as one who had worked closely with Knutson during the days when both of them had been active in the ministry to students, Heiges as executive secretary of the Division of College and University Work, National Lutheran Council, and Knutson as president of the Lutheran Student Association of America. From this association had grown a mutuality of respect and Heiges recalled: "I not only came to admire you greatly but I also came to the conviction that someday you would be an outstanding leader in the church."

The letters, papers, and reports from Knutson's days as a student leader adumbrated the Heiges prophecy. One example will suffice. As president of the LSAA during the years 1950-1951, it fell to his lot to chair the annual meeting of the Lutheran Student Council of America, held August 22-25, 1951 at Interlachen, Michigan. The minutes of that meeting, including the agenda and the president's report, reveal a striking similarity to later reports he was to make as the president of The American Lutheran Church. It began quite properly with an introduction that promised an accounting of his stewardship. This was fourfold: first, a bird's eye view of the Lutheran Student Movement; second, a report of his administration of national activities; third, a delineation of future hopes; and fourth, a list of presidential recommendations for adoption. The last two sections are of special importance for us in discerning the mind of this young leader. He reminded his audience that the Student Volunteer Movement Quadrennial would be occurring shortly and that Christian students had long been in the forefront of the missionary enterprise of the church. He expected that the LSAA would send 300 students to the SVM meeting on the campus of the University of Kansas at Lawrence.

Moreover, he urged students to try to attend and participate in the Lutheran World Federation Assembly (Hannover, 1952). "We hope that at least 100 students will go," he said. Closely related to this expectation was Knutson's high evaluation of the ecumenical movement and his encouragement of greater participation by Lutherans who had much to learn and much to give.

Finally, he recommended that the executive committee conduct a study conference in 1951-52 to examine the relationship of the LSAA to the university and to consider the possibility of a full-time LSAA president. He said this was necessary if there was "to be real leadership and expansion into new areas." The president's job he said, was "a very taxing one." Whoever he would be, the president must be given time and resources for his role as leader.

In the light of subsequent developments, it is clear that already as a student, Knutson had the ability to create a climate of confidence among his peers and to stimulate them to both thought and action. He never underestimated the potential of a community of believers. He held before them high but not impossible expectations. One must conclude, therefore, that here was a leader who analyzed accurately current circumstances in the light of history and personal experience and then, possessed with remarkable perception, was able to help his co-workers to visualize the future. There is nothing particularly exciting or noteworthy about a person who has 20/20 hindsight, but, when a man appears on the scene and demonstrates an almost unfailing 20/20 foresight, then it is time to quote Mordecai's question to Queen Esther: "Who knows whether you have not come to the kingdom for such a time as this?" This text, incidentally, was one of Knutson's favorites and he gave numerous addresses using this topic as a point of departure.

Kent Knutson had been elected president of Wartburg in 1968. In 1970, the first president of The American Lutheran Church, Fredrik A. Schiotz, was scheduled for retirement. Schiotz, like Knutson, had been closely identified with the student movement since 1922 (he was the second president of the LSAA), and moreover, he had been a helpful counselor when Knutson was experiencing his vocational struggle, something that had begun indeed prior to those decisive days in Whiting, Indiana at the Standard Oil refinery. With Schiotz's retirement imminent, it was only natural that widespread speculation occurred as to his successor. Among the names most frequently mentioned were those of some district presidents, some theological professors (one had unapologetically declared himself openly a candidate on the thesis that politics in the church affairs should be overt rather than covert), and some parish pastors. Among the latter was David W. Preus, vice-president of The American Lutheran Church and a Minneapolis clergyman, whose name had been to the fore at least since 1968 when the church began to think about its next chief executive.

Election procedures required that the districts of The American Lutheran Church participate in the process of nomination and that from the names submitted those ten receiving the most frequent affirmation would constitute the slate of nominees to be voted on by the general convention at San Antonio, Texas, in October, 1970. Knutson was among these ten.

An additional feature of the election procedure was a short public statement by each nominee prior to the election. Knutson's statement dealt with the gospel, the identity and mission of the church, Lutheran unity (he predicted its achievement in the 1970s), and a ministerial rather than magisterial administration. He cited his experience as professor, administrator, and ecumenical churchman, and then concluded: "If you should be led to choose me for this task, I shall serve you with all the energy and wisdom at my command. If you should choose another, I shall continue to serve in my place with the same energy and with joy. So choose, calmly, carefully and with confidence. May God's Spirit be with you."

The election occurred on October 23, 1970, and Knutson emerged as the choice of the church on the third ballot. Among many quotable paragraphs, Knutson's acceptance speech included two or three that were characteristically "grace-full" and simple. Regarding the second runner (whom the convention later chose to be vice-president), Knutson said: "David Preus was my colleague in my seminary days, and I have been close to him in the ministry ever since. He was my pastor for a time when I was on the faculty at Luther Seminary in St. Paul. He and I exchanged good greetings of fellowship before this convention opened. . . . I would have been happy to have followed him as [our] president, and he has said that also about your decision." He then turned to the question of Lutheran unity and said "I pledge myself to work with [other American and world Lutherans] as closely as it is humanly possible, and by the guidance of God's Spirit to come to a very much closer unity in the years ahead." He was on record as seeing its realization within a decade. What he did not publicly express was his dismay at developments within the Missouri Synod that would make the realization of his hope all but impossible. Then, after touching on the ecumenical question and the current problems in a depressed and suffering world, he declared his personal faith by confessing Luther's explanation of the Apostles' Creed, emphasizing, "I cannot by my own reason or strength believe in Jesus Christ . . . , but the Holy Spirit has called me by the gospel." He concluded: "God does not promise us everything. . . . But he does promise us that he will give us grace to trust him, and this is the splendor of the church. . . . I live and work in the light of that grace." On this note he took office as the second president of The American Lutheran Church January 1, 1971.

How does one "take over" a high office? What does a president do the first days behind a new desk? Knutson decided he would begin by avoiding the desk for a short while. With his wife, Norma, accompanying him, he made unhurried visits to the various departments of the national offices and the closely associated Augsburg Publishing House. The casual nature of the visits was disarming, yet purposeful. The new president entered the small office of a secretary not as a mighty bureaucrat with the mien of an inquisitor, but as a friend and learner. After shaking hands and asking the name of the worker, and something about the person's home and family, he often would inquire about the nature of the individual's particular task. How was her or his work related to the whole enterprise of the church? In recalling this, Norma said, "We shook the hand of every secretary, errand boy, mail clerk, and executive in those two buildings." When he finished the tour, he came back to his office, sat down at his desk, and with a wry sense of humor said, "I wonder what a church president is supposed to do. Well, I guess I'll begin by reading my mail." He quickly discovered the awesome responsibilities of his new office, and this discovery kept him working until he entered the hospital in October, 1972.

We have neither the space nor the inclination to chronicle the life and activity of Kent Knutson as president of one of the three major Lutheran bodies in America. *What* he did, *how* he did it, and, most important of all, *why* he did it are topics for an in-depth study by some future interpreter of the life and work of the ALC's second president. What we need now is a quick summary of those months from January 1971 to his death in March, 1973, a summary pointing out that many of the main emphases of his previous years now found an arena in which he could focus his deep spiritual and theological convictions, his keen analysis of the human predicament, and his wise judgment of what the people of God were obligated and empowered to do in this age.

His mind and his activities, including thousands of miles of travel in the USA and around the world, roamed over the vast interlocking network of men and institutions that constituted an evangelical catholic church in mission to the world. Overshadowing the daily office routine, the relationship to colleagues in the national offices, the concern for congregations, pastors, and district presidents, colleges, seminaries, campus and other specialized ministries, Lutheran unity, ecumenical dialogue, and social action was his growing and passionate zeal for communicating the Word of God. In fact, by his own admission—in a sort of "how-my-mind-has-changed" statement—he confessed that his earlier theological priorities needed reordering. In the foreword to a 1972 publication *(Lutheranism in North America 1914-1970)* he wrote: "I have often said that the real question facing us is not 'What is the gospel,' but rather, 'What is the church,' that is, what is the purpose, the mission and task of the church. This now has been demonstrated to be too simplistic. I still affirm that the Lutheran understanding of the gospel is clearly taught and held. . . . But I cannot any longer assume that the faith that is taught has been appropriated in the congregation to the degree it must if we are to remain the church of the Reformation."

Having recognized this fact of ecclesiastical life among Lutherans, it was not strange that his first (and alas, his last) presidential report delivered to The American Lutheran Church in October, 1972, carried these strong words:

> The articulation of the faith is desperately important in an increasingly secularized society. All of us must bend greater efforts to speak the gospel clearly, concisely, firmly, and lovingly. . . . The gospel never changes. The classical tradition of Christendom, especially as embodied in our own Lutheran Confessions, are for me the basis for this witness. This glorious expression of faith which enlivened the church in the past lives on to inspire and to instruct us. We must never allow our tradition to become deadened by our inability to compre-

> hend its richness or to become romanticized by a mere formal acquiescence. The question is not whether we have the gospel. The question is only whether we have fully understood and proclaimed it.

The weeks and months between his election to office and his death were filled to overflowing. The summer and autumn of 1972 were inordinately busy. The schedule called for a world-circling trip that included the Far East, the Middle East, and Europe.

The air ticket showed stops at Tokyo, Seoul, Hong Kong, Medan and Djakarta (Indonesia), Sydney, Adelaide, Brisbane (all in Australia), Port Moresby and Lae (in New Guinea), Taipei (Taiwan), Singapore, Madras, Delhi, Tel Aviv, Frankfurt, Amsterdam, New York, and then back to Minneapolis. Accompanied by his wife, he began the long and exhausting journey on July 2 and returned on August 23. The trip had grown out of his official duty to attend the meeting of the Executive Committee of the Lutheran World Federation in July, being held in Sumatra, Indonesia, with the local Batak Church as host; and the regular meeting of the Central Committee of the World Council of Churches, convening in August in Utrecht, Holland. What better opportunity would there be to acquaint himself with the overseas work of the church? Thus the trip became an intensive visitation of Lutheran churches in parts of the world hitherto not visited.

Although he was deeply involved and intensely interested in the official LWF and WCC meetings, his later comments revealed that for him and Mrs. Knutson the opportunity to visit the Christians of a non-Western culture was the most disturbing part of the many-faceted experience. Intellectually and emotionally this first hand encounter with the far-flung missions of the church was overwhelming in its impact; it was more than he could assimilate. However, with an insatiable curiosity about people, their life, and their customs—religious, social, political—Knutson revelled in each new circumstance. He became a devourer of impressions, filing them away in his capacious mind and yearning for more. Each day required an astonishing expenditure of energy, so much that in hindsight there remains the lurking question: was the pace too taxing even for this physically strong man? Did the long days, difficult travel, strange food and drink leave him vulnerable to the encroachment of a resident or alien death-dealing virus? Both Dr. and Mrs. Knutson came down with colds, moving as they did from tropically hot, humid locations to the chill of mountainous highlands.

It was in India that Knutson developed a symptom that physicians of the world-renowned Mayo Clinic subsequently identified as the first sign of the disease that was to take his life. He began to toss about in bed. Though exhausted, he could not sleep. Involuntary twitching movements of the body kept him awake and served only to increase the enervation. "The last enemy" was beginning the attack.

Upon returning to America, he was immediately thrust into the preparatory work for the sixth general convention of The American Lutheran Church, scheduled to be held October 4-10, 1972, in Minneapolis. In the introduction to his presidential report, he said, "I aim to enjoy this convention. We are about work we all love and with people we all recognize as friends and co-workers. What could be more fun! Let's enjoy it together!" He was relaxed because he was convinced that God spoke through the church, that the church was God's not his. Then he proceeded in systematic fashion to explain to the delegates "how the convention works." Part two he entitled, "The State of the Church"; part three was a report of the ALC at work, concentrating on areas for which the president had particular responsibility; and fourth, the report concluded with

Knutson's proposals for restructuring the national offices of the church. The latter was the continuation of a study begun in 1966 by the establishment of a long Range Study Committee, which by 1968 had been altered to a smaller continuation Long Range Study Committee that brought a report to the 1970 convention. Although some of the 1970 recommendations were adopted, the newly elected president asked the convention to defer action until 1972, thus giving him time to comprehend this inherited task and to relate the structural changes to his style of leadership and the needs of the church as he saw them. After long deliberation and discussion in the intervening months, he made his proposals. Of major importance in understanding his concept of structure it is well to look at Knutson's basic assumptions rather than the details of reorganization. The ease of the structural transition was to be facilitated immeasurably by his adherence to these principles. They were five in number:

(1) Structural change must improve functional effectiveness;

(2) The Church constantly faces new challenges in a changing world;

(3) Mutuality is a key to understanding the polity of the ALC;

(4) The value of existing structures must be recognized and a concern for continuity must be exercised;

(5) Structural change should not deter progress toward Lutheran unity.

He closed his report with what he deemed a "marvelous idea." Although biennial conventions are necessary, they do not and cannot involve each congregation. Such a convention would be too large and cumbersome. Therefore, to enhance the feeling of participation, he proposed that once a decade there be an "Assembly of Congregations," a large meeting that would bring together representatives of all the congregations for inspirational and informational purposes. If a suitable site could be secured (he had in mind Washington, D.C.), the first such assembly might be held in the American Bicentennial Year of 1976.

Knutson presided over the convention with consummate skill, firmness, good humor, and impartiality. It was a virtuoso performance. Nobody realized that the president suffered spells of dizziness, twitching, and coughing. Moreover he had become conscious of a strange feeling around his eyes. At times, this master of articulation had to search for words, an impairment that was not noticed by his listeners. One of the highlights of the convention was to be a Sunday night public rally devoted to the task of evangelism in the contemporary world. The prominent Indonesian Christian leader, Dr. Soritu Nababan was scheduled to speak. When it became necessary for him to cancel his appearance, Dr. Philip Potter, general secretary of the World Council of Churches, accepted the assignment only to learn a short time later that a prior commitment made it necessary for him to be in London. Confronted by what threatened to collapse the program, Knutson sought the advice of friends. Finally, the suggestion that he himself deliver the address, a recommendation made by persons ignorant that a fatal disease had already taken hold of him, was accepted. Thus it came about that Knutson's last address dealt with one of the major themes that occupied his mind: the gospel and its proclamation by the church to the world. The address was entitled, "A New Look at Evangelism."

The day after the convention, he turned to the Knutson family doctor for wide-scale tests hoping to diagnose his rapidly growing speech impairment. After transfer to the Mayo Clinic in Rochester, Minnesota, he underwent further tests, but his speech and memory continued to deteriorate. One by one the disease possibilities were eliminated until finally the physicians reached the unhappy conclusion that he was victim of a bizarre disorder of the central nervous system, the Jacob-Creutzfeldt disease. "There is no known treatment that would alter (its) course," said the Mayo doctors. "It is characterized by a gradual loss of intellectual functions such as memory and the ability to speak, loss of muscular coordination, and involuntary muscular jerking. Usually, death occurs from several months to a year or two after the onset of the disease."

After thirteen weeks of treatment, Knutson was returned to a Minneapolis hospital. Seven weeks later, on March 12, 1973, he died.

Was death on his mind? Yes, it had to be, because as a Christian theologian, he knew death as the last enemy. He declared at the funeral of his friend and colleague, William Larsen, "I am angry that sin and death stalk man. A righteous anger, I pray, that will not be quiet when men suffer and die. I am comforted only with the knowledge that God is angry too! So angry that he submitted himself to the same suffering and death and overcame the enemy with his power and gives us the fruits of his victory."

Yes, he had intimations of death. In a Lenten book *(God's Drama in Seven Acts,* pp. 45-46) he wrote, "After Jesus' final work, there was silence . . . He died. Silence is the dreadful enemy of man. Death and silence are much the same. Even evil, judgment, and hurt are preferable, for they speak. They are alive. They pay attention to us, seek us out, confirm our identity. . . . Man is not a man unless he expresses himself, unless he speaks. . . . A man is born to speak and to hear." The gift of speech, the gift of intelligent communication, this was a mark of human life. Now, Kent Knutson was struck speechless. "Could any enemy," asked Alvin Rogness, "strike with more cunning, leering at having first destroyed the superb gift of communication which God had given this man, and then watching him reach out in futility to those he loved? And meanwhile a whole church waiting in prayer, bewildered, sometimes angry, hoping against hope for the turn that did not come."

What diabolical craftiness! What demonic irony! The enemy had struck at Kent's greatest strengths: intellect and speech. He who placed such high value on communicating the Word by which God had broken the silence of the world, was now robbed of the gift of words and finally of life itself.

But he who died still speaks to us. Paradoxically the speechless one has not been silenced; he charges those who still have the gift of speech in the midst of the world's raucous, noisy, and explosive silence to hear the Word that breaks all silence. His friend and ours, St. Paul, said "So truth comes from what is heard, and what is heard comes by the preaching of Christ" (Rom. 10:17). Therefore he who has ears to hear let him hear!

VI

What should the reader "hear" as he reads the following selections from Knutson's works? What were the main ideas that energized this energetic man? What were the overriding emphases that absorbed his attention as he responded to the Word which he had heard?

Nothing would be more appropriate than to begin with his personal piety, his love of family, and his concern for persons young and old. Two of his writings, *His Only Son our Lord* and *God's Drama in Seven Acts* are especially rich in references to his personal faith. Here is but one among many:

> Jesus Christ is the ultimate reality for me. When I call him Lord I attribute to him absolute mastery over my life, my possessions, my hopes, my fears. He is my God. He is a present living reality. I pray to him, give him my adoration and praise, and center my understanding of myself and the world in him. . . . Jesus died for me. This is the

> faith. God does not promise a paradise on earth—indeed, he indicates that evil shall continue, even accelerate, but the ultimate end is clear, for God shall triumph as he has shown us in the victory of the resurrection. *(His Only Son Our Lord,* pp. 96, 79, 110).

It was this personal piety that permeated the Knutson family life. It was natural, not forced or artificial. Parents and children were at ease with one another in the joys of the Lord. There was piety, but no legalistic pietism.

One of the last things that the dying father did was to write individual letters to his six children. This was accomplished only with extreme difficulty and a losing battle for coherent expression. His letter to Kris on October 27, 1972, shows both the deep love and the poignant struggle:

> Dear Kris,
>
> You are the growing young man that I hope I had always hoped [sic]. I cannot hope anything more could have ~~here have~~ [sic] given me. A nothing more precious could be given. . . . Thanks [sic] you for the wonderful years you have given me.
>
> Ephesians 1:7-9 Dad

This piety found expression in concern for all manner of people, but especially the distressed and lonely. Norma Knutson said that Kent tried not to bring his problems home with him, but more than once he produced from his brief case a pitiful letter from a financially or emotionally desperate pastor's widow, or some deeply disturbed layman wondering about "what was happening to spiritual life in the church." Each of these voices from within the community of faith received his personal and often lengthy consideration. After all, these were persons for whom Christ had won the great victory, and he as a shepherd must care for his sheep.

How he enjoyed his family! The gathering of the clan in Eagle Grove, Iowa, to celebrate Christmas; the pleasures of children in birthday parties; the shared joy of playing games. What a contrast to a famous European theologian, whose son reported that his father, a theological giant, regularly set aside one day a year to play with his children, and then he always saw to it that he won the games!

Second, the reader of these writings will be made aware—he will "hear"—the throbbing theological mind at work. Knutson penetrated the deepest theological questions and yet had the gift to express them in a manner that the less gifted and the untutored could grasp. He had scorn for those who avoided the rigors of disciplined thought, but great sympathy for the weak in faith and the struggling doubter. At an early stage in his development he told me that his theology was quite simple. In fact, it could be summarized in the final sentence of Herbert Butterfield's *Christianity and History:* "Hold to Christ, and for the rest be totally uncommitted." Later he learned that this could be quite misleading and even dangerously simplistic. The more he studied classical Christian theology the more convinced he became that the faith of the church must be a spoken, confessed faith. Thus *confessional* theology occupied his thought. As the presiding bishop of the church, he wrote in his report of 1971 ("The State of the Church: Hope and Anxiety"): "The Lutheran confessions define and preserve the gospel in a way which is unparalleled in Christian history." This was no appeal to repristinate or parrot the words of the confessions, for that would be to call attention to the confessions themselves. His conviction lay in this that the confessions were not "self-conscious" but "evangel-conscious," the church's great safeguard to the proclamation of the gospel.

Third, the reader should "hear" the sounds of a broad-ranging churchmanship, a churchmanship informed by piety, theology, and practical sagacity. And it began in the congregation. He understood that it was in the local parish that the most intimate experiences and highest expressions of "the communion of the Holy Spirit" occurred. Moreover, the life in the parish and the ministry of the pastor were indivisible. Hence his abiding preoccupation with the doctrine of the ministry, and the preparation of students for this ministry. "Tell me about your ministry," he said to a co-worker in the national office. The reply was: "Four parishes, twenty-six years, all very special, and I had a great experience in each!" Knutson's response was deliberate and straight: "I want you to say that over and over again, a thousand thousand times, wherever and whenever you have the chance."

But despite his high evaluation of the congregation, he was not a congregationalist. He saw the church as the New Testament depicted it, as possessing both a particular (local) and a universal aspect (note Chapter 5 in *The Shape of the Question*). The church was the people of God, the body of Christ, finding historical expression wherever the Word was proclaimed and the sacraments administered in harmony with that Word. And this manifestation of the church was not confined to the parish. It was present at all levels, regional, national, and global, each involving a sociological dimension or structure appropriate to its most effective functional purposes. The church must always be in mission, for it is "sent" into this age. But the form of the church must always facilitate the mission. This, of course, lay at the root of his concern for restructuring the ALC national offices.

Fourth, the reader should "hear" his understanding of the role of the church in education. While parish education was basic for him, the church directed his energies primarily into higher education. It was only natural that a former theological professor and seminary president should occupy himself with the problems and concerns of those institutions preparing men and women for the ministry. His high view of the ministry could only lead to deep convictions regarding theological education. More surprising, however, was the fact that this man, a product of a state university and dedicated to the campus ministries at tax-supported schools, gave himself so unstintingly to the colleges of the church. In an address to representatives of the colleges (April 7, 1972) he said:

> I believe that the church college is a Christian community with a mission. It is the church at a particular place doing a particular kind of mission. It is a church living on the frontiers of culture. . . . The church college and the church belong together . . . the church college needs the church, as well as the church needs the church college.

Without strong, healthy, far-sighted, and evangelical educational institutions the church would soon be bereft of the kind of leaders that the mission of the church in a secular age required. But open to the gifts of God, he said, the church can serve with readiness in any age and face any task in each generation.

Finally, the reader should "hear" his continuing call for church unity. It was no idle or perfunctory recitation when he confessed the Nicene Creed: "I believe in *one,* holy, catholic, and apostolic church." There was no question in his mind that unity is a mark of the church. The people of God are one, the body of Christ is one. The huge problem was the invariable and historical difficulty of manifesting before the world this already given unity. The fragmentation of Christendom into separate and often competing bodies was a scandal (in the New Testament sense of the word as offense) to the world, an obstacle to the mission of the church as expressed by Jesus in John 17: ". . . that the world may believe that thou hast sent me . . . that the world may know that thou hast sent me and hast loved them even as thou hast loved me." For Kent Knutson this meant unceasing effort to help the church understand the unitive power of the gospel. Unity in the congregations, unity in the church over which he presided, unity among Lutherans in America and the world, unity among Christians everywhere—this was the goal. But it was never to be a unity by compromise nor was it to be unity the requirements of which went beyond the Lutheran confession: "For it is sufficient for the true unity of the Christian church that the gospel be preached in conformity with a pure understanding of it and the sacraments be administered in accordance with the divine Word." (Augsburg Confession, Art. VII, Tappert, *Book of Concord,* p. 32). Ever since his student days in the Lutheran Student Association of America, he had been gripped by this goal and he dedicated himself to its furtherance. He was impatient with church leaders of limited vision and either flabby or rigid theologies that failed to push to the evangelical heart of the confessions. When his efforts and those of his friends were censured as the activities of "self-appointed critics," he was grieved, not because of a personal affront, but because of this display of theological mediocrity.

Closely related to this was his involvement in what came to be known as "the ecumenical dialogue." Of particular importance were his contributions in the Roman Catholic-Lutheran conversations after Vatican II. From one point of view, his lecture at the Lutheran World Assembly at Evian, France (1970) together with that of Jan Cardinal Willibrands, chairman of the Vatican's Secretariat for the Promotion of Christian Unity, was a highwater mark. The esteem of both the Roman Catholic Church and the World Council of Churches for Knutson was attested by the presence at his funeral of a high ranking member of the Catholic hierarchy in

America, and the written tribute of Dr. Philip Potter, the General Secretary of the World Council. Said he:

> In his relatively short span of service to the ecumenical movement, Kent Knutson made an amazingly mature contribution. . . . We trust the Lord to raise up other Lutherans to replace the Frys and Knutsons who have been taken from us.

So, in summary, here are some of the things to listen for as you read: the sounds from a loving and loyal son of devout, immigrant parents; the echoes of joy reverberating in a home where he was a happy and loving husband and father; the pastoral concern in parish, seminary, and presidential office; the evidences of a brilliant mind and a sharply honed intellect; and the warm evangelical outreach of a churchman for whom the gospel was, in Luther's words, "the true treasure of the church."

E. Clifford Nelson

Gospel

Bible

The Scriptures are empowered by God's own power. They have authority that we dare not diminish nor could we if we dared. But it is an authority which invites involvement, which wants us to become so immersed that his gift of grace reaches out and grasps us. The Bible is not a dead instrument to which we give intellectual assent. It is God we deal with in the Bible and not bare facts.[152] *

The American Lutheran Church believes that the Bible is the Word of God and is therefore the only infallible authority in all matters of faith and life. This written Word of God is at the center of the church's life, in preaching, in teaching, in witnessing, in worship and is applicable to all moral questions and decisions. The American Lutheran Church accepts and confesses the Lutheran Confessions as found in the Book of Concord and requires sub-

* The numbers following each quotation refer to the source in the bibliography chronologically and numbered consecutively. Each item has a number and the footnote number is the number of the source in the bibliography. Where two items have the same date a significant letter from the title has been added for easy identification. We are indebted to Robert Wiederaenders and Mrs. Juel Pierce for compiling this complete bibliography.

scription to them of all its members, both congregations and individuals.[83]

I think that we are really the products of American experience in more ways than we really understand ourselves. We have been cast into a kind of a role by the kind of debate which has been going on around us on the outside. We have been maneuvered into the kind of position where the formality of scripture, that is, the authority of scripture itself, has become that about which we debate rather than the content of the scripture, rather than the witness of the scripture, rather than the revelation which the scripture brings to us. And this in a certain sense—and I must say this quite carefully and qualifiedly because it is not true in all senses—but in a certain sense this is not a Lutheran question. This is a Reformed question. This is the Fundamentalist-Liberal question. This is the kind of a question which grew out of a different strain of the Reformation than the Lutheran strain. So I say that it is a bit strange, but that of course doesn't change the necessity for engaging in discussion about it because if someone raises the question it deserves an answer.[84]

Confession

I love the dogmas of the church. I endorse the confessions of the church. I insist that my students know them well. But I am convinced that theology is not the formulation of certain principles that go on and on without change. Preaching is not simply the restatement of accepted doctrines. If you simply repeat again and again the language of another age, no matter how correctly or how meticulously, you will not have fulfilled your task of making Jesus Lord today in the life and in the understanding of the modern world. Theology is the living reinterpretation of Christ's Lordship for every age.[18]

The identity of the church resides in its Confessions. The Lutheran Confessions provide to us

styles of life

what a person is

a shape for living

a guarantee of freedom—the gospel is to be communicated in such a way as to free us

an understanding of response which is world-oriented

a confession of the gospel which is catholic in its thrust—one gospel unites

leads to new obedience—doing the gospel[103]

Confession

For me, the Lutheran confessions are the proper and sufficient exposition of God's revelation in Scripture and I take my stand with them. I regard my task to speak this Gospel in a language which communicates itself to this generation in this time. To understand and accept the Lutheran confessions is not simply to tape them or to reiterate them, but it is to take the challenge which is in them and to put that challenge to work, both in the deeds required for our time and in the language which communicates in our time.[86]

Death

We know that we shall die. Indeed, the most certain thing about our life is our death. Our death will be an eschaton, a fulfillment, in the future. God will consummate his purposes, and one phase of our existence will come to a final end at a particular moment. Our destination in this sense is well known to us. It probably is involved in either our unconscious or conscious thinking every waking moment.

God will call us at death and give us new life, just as he raised Jesus from the dead, so he will raise us up. Then he will judge us. This will not be a new judgment for we will have been judged all along. Nor will it be a surprising judgment for those who have loved him, for the promise of the Gospel has already told us of the meaning of that reception.[160]

Death has many faces. As a fleeting image it conveys comfort for it is a release from pain and sometimes from loneliness and despair. . . . At its root, behind the masks, death is an enemy. It is a product of evil and sin. It is our last enemy, in the words of St. Paul.

Death is not to be accepted as much as it is to be overcome. . . . I am angry that sin and death stalk man—a righteous anger, I pray, that will not be quiet when men suffer and die. I am comforted only with the knowledge that God is angry too. So angry that he submitted himself to the same suffering and death and overcame this enemy with his power and gives to us the fruits of his victory. He has invited us to share in his death and resurrection.[160]

Faith

It is you he loves. And if you are to know his love, if you are to celebrate and enjoy his love, you must trust it. Faith does not create grace. God does not love you because you believe it. But he wants you to become aware of his love, that's faith, trust his love, that's faith, respond to his love, that's faith, [be] grateful for his love, that's faith. They go together, grace alone and faith alone.[154]

The Message

The Gospel thus has empirical elements, an interpreted claim, and an embodiment in living expression. The Gospel cannot be defined only in terms of historical events or confessional ideas or ethical norms or mystical experiences and it is equally clear that it belongs to both the past the present and thus by its nature involves us in the question of the constant and the changing.[162]

There is nothing as embracing in its consequence for this world or for you than that which we called the gospel. You are saved by that gospel, and you are made free for this world by this gospel. Until every man is free, until every man is saved, our task, my task, your task is to live by and for that gospel.[141]

Incarnation

That God became man, which is one of the ways we speak of the incarnation, is a compliment to man which restores his faith in himself. Man is not to be something else than what he is but he is to be restored to that which he was created to be.[124]

Jesus Christ

I greet you in the name of our Lord Jesus Christ. May his power, his patience, and his abundant hope stir you and shape you to his service.[120]

My first purpose will be to honor Jesus Christ. He is the cause of all my striving, the center of all my thinking, and the source of all my loving. He is my joy and hope for all mankind. He gives me strength to do my task. He gives me courage to stand against those, in and out of the Church, who seek to tear it down. He gives me patience to endure the pressure, and whatever wisdom, if any, I possess.[86]

Justice

We have, in fact, in times and places in modern times wiped out whole peoples. Systematically, scientifically, deliberately. To that the church should say no.[140]

Man/Woman

The self is like a forest with many entities, many trees, which act like separate selves—the will, the wind, the heart, ambition, anxiousness, fear, ego, joy, boredom, desires, depression, envy, loneliness, longing, fulfillment—the moods, the drives come and go in an everlasting and illogical sequence. You're a wonderful creature and yet fearful and unpredictable. There seems to be no center to us, no controlling point, no inherent shape or pattern.[138]

We are made free to be human.[141]

And we have used this concept of total depravity to depress man, to destroy him in order to save him and we have equated very nearly the source of evil and men.[124]

Man cannot escape despair. Only when he faces up to the realities of his enemies—of death, of suffering, of ignorance, of hopelessness—only when he faces these can he attain clarity as to his task and achieve sufficient confidence to live. The reality of evil is a necessary theme in understanding the Reformation thrust. For unless one takes seriously evil, one does not understand his mission, one does not understand what man is, one does not understand what man should do.[124]

A man is a man is a man and he is a man to be identified with mankind and it is with men as mankind that God has chosen to deal.[124]

Man is too clever and too demonic to play God. In the process he destroys both himself and God.[124]

People of God

The American Lutheran Church understands itself to be the people of God and belonging to the whole people of God on earth. In its own life, it views the congregation, which is Church in its fullness, as "the basic but not the only manifestation of the Body of Christ. As a union of congregations, The ALC is also the Church. The constitution describes the relationship between the congregation and The ALC as one of mutuality. This also applies to other expressions of the Church in conferences, districts, and other structures. Each has a responsibility to the others, is dependent on them and is necessary to fulfill the mission God has given us.[63]

Resurrection

Jesus Christ without resurrection is not the Christ of the Christian faith. A blatant statement which requires interpretation! I understand the resurrection to mean that Christ has been made Lord, that is, he has been made the universal authority and hope for man. The particularity of the Jew who lived in Palestine has been universalized to be the Gospel for all men everywhere.[162]

To say Jesus Christ rose from the dead is to say that he reigns as Lord. There may be more which can be said but it may not be necessary to say more. But to say this *is* necessary.[162]

Easter is the celebration of Christ's victory and his exaltation to Lordship. Enjoy your Easter joy—help your people enjoy it. Easter is a day for the Gospel—no Law preaching on that day, please—no proving of the resurrection, no scolding, no intellectual puzzle solving, but proclamation of a great hope. And what a great hope it is![126]

Theology

If you're going to have a good theological debate you might as well have it on something which is important.[132]

But if we are going to think through a particular theological issue, I hope in our day with the pressures about us we will do it on a fundamental issue and not a peripheral one, not choose some small historical detail lying thousands of years back in history and try to resurrect something which is beyond our capacity to do. But we really rather talk about that which affects us now, that witness and power of God as it expresses itself in that form of his word.[132]

I am always glad to find someone against anti-intellectualism. I am very unhappy to find someone anti-intellectual.[124]

In the church that lives by the gospel theological education needs to be central.[127]

Unity

The unity of the church was our main theme and when we spoke of fellowship we meant the fellowship among Christians. But now the question of the division of the world and the unity of mankind have come before us with tremendous force. For many the unity of mankind has become more important than the unity of the church. John Deschner last night talked about the church as being a sign or sacrament of the coming unity of mankind, and that struck a very responsive note with many of you. Yet there are some of you who would raise questions about that and who would rather speak of the integrity of the world in which God is operating, an integrity which is its own and in which all men participate fully, Christian or not.[150]

Church

Change

Structural change must improve functional effectiveness. The apparent desire of the Church for new structures is wholesome if its intention is to develop greater effectiveness in achieving its mission. Structures must always be subservient to mission. The basic emphasis is therefore on function rather than the structure itself.

The Church constantly faces new challenges in a changing world. While the gospel and the basic mission of the Church do not change, the continuing changes in our society confront us with new opportunities, possibilities, and problems. We must be ready to adjust our structures from time to time because the situation into which God sends us changes and because through experience we may become wiser.

The gospel can be served well by any number of structural arrangements. There can be no final or perfect structure. Let no one believe that the Church was wrong before or that we are now about to finish the debate.[127]

We have indicated that there can be no change in the first priority of proclaiming and acting out the Gospel. That is what makes the Church the Church. We have no other reason for existence.

But God may be leading us to "do" the Gospel with particular emphases in our time. We must discover his leading.

I believe that we must continually be open to new paths. We should discover those particular tasks that we are to do in our time. The church in America has now become a church in diaspora—a mission church. We are no longer the "establishment"—if we ever were. Our task is not too different from the church in other lands across the seas. To discover this mission, to carry out this task of evangelism, to communicate the enthusiasm and the insights and to implement the organizational forms to do this mission may be that priority which we have yet to articulate.[104]

New structures grow out of old structures. The Church has traditions in its procedures which have imbued wisdom. One changes them only with great care. Any proposal for change should pay great attention to smooth transition so that the mission of the Church is not disrupted or lessened in its impact.[127]

We work in a new society—one characterized by crisis, secularization, change. There is urgency for us to deal with hard realities, not just what we would like it to be. In this context the church faces a struggle for its survival.[34]

Community

One of the keys to applying the inter-action principle is the understanding of the church. The church, as understood in our tradition, is a community. It is a holy community in which the Gospel is preached and the sacraments are administered. The institutional forms through which this community seeks to express itself may and do vary, but these forms are to a large degree irrelevant insofar as the essential nature of the community is concerned. This community is always a part of a larger community, called society. By society I mean that vast array of routine and complex sets of human relationships in which every person participates. It includes family, job, school, leisure and local, state, national, and international levels. It has aspects we call race, class, economic levels, emotional planes, age, sex, education, opportunity, geography, time, and health.

These two communities, the Christian community and society, are not mutually exclusive or easily distinguishable. They are very nearly completely intermingled. The Christian is a member of society even within his Christian community. He cannot easily separate the two in either function or thought.[34]

Congregation

The national Church is subject to the collective will of the congregations, and the congregations are responsible to receive services from, to utilize possibilities provided by, and to cooperate with the collective will.

Mutuality in mission can be a great strength for a Church. It precludes both selfish, independence, and autocratic leadership. It creates the context for responsible freedom. It is a great joy to live and work in a community of trust and sharing.[127]

Christianity and Culture

Lutherans are people who live in a culture of a time and place, whatever that culture may be, and who, in that place, have been grasped by a faith which is not a product of that environment but rather mediated through it. By understanding this, and its attendant dangers, the Gospel as we understand, it can survive. Perhaps it can survive better than in a culture where the human commitment to one view of reality forces the understanding of the faith to conform, reform and perhaps be deformed.[63]

Diversity

It is no secret that the Lutheran tradition, the great theological tradition of the Western world, is a long and complicated tradition of a number of theological strains. And that's part of the richness of the Lutheran heritage, and a part of the freedom and the diverse possibilities in the Lutheran tradition. We should not be worried about that, nor should we be particularly surprised about it.[132]

Faithfulness

When I came back from San Antonio, the students and faculty at Wartburg Seminary met me at the airport with banners and a brass band. They presented me with a gift—a black iron weather vane rooster—a replica of the one at the top of the Wartburg tower. I had used that cock as an illustration in my speech at San Antonio for it has been a constant reminder to me of Peter and his denial of his Lord. Now it hangs in my office and each day I am reminded that I live by grace alone and that faithfulness is a gift to be cherished. I hope that each of you lives by that grace. All of the Christian virtues issue from that understanding.[81]

Fallibility

The American Lutheran Church can err. The Lutheran Church—Missouri Synod can err. What shall we do when we both act out of our conviction that this is what the Bible teaches? We live together and seek greater wisdom. Let us not act hastily in judging one another without listening to one another. We believe God's grace is great enough for us to live together in the freedom he has granted us.[130]

Hope

My eschatology is not quantitative or time bound but rather a "transcendent" dimension in life which permits me to live in trust and hope without any crutch—be it my own improvement or some renewal of the church. What if the church were not renewed? Has then God failed us or have we failed him? Not necessarily either. This would mean only that the absurdity of the human condition is reflected also in the church. The church is none other than the human condition believing and hoping as it continues in its absurdity.[161]

Wondering.... How we are going to end the year on our stewardship. Remember that it will take 6.1 percent increase in congregational giving to make it. We are now doing between 4 and 5 percent. Not bad, but not good enough. We have a very small increase planned for 1973. Can you come through now with 2 or 3 percent more? It would be really something to go over the top this year!

Where my son is going to college next year. That will mean two in college for the next ten years! (And then comes Karl! Can't imagine him in college. . . .)

If the two apple trees I planted will make it all the way to good apples one fall. Isn't it great to plant a tree? [157]

Lord's Supper

The Lord's Supper is Gospel, not Law. As Baptism, the Supper must be understood as God's gracious gift to men. It is grace. The purpose is not to demand but to give, not to divide but to unify, not to judge, but to comfort, not to bring sorrow, but joy. The gift is *for* man and his salvation. It is not designed to strike men's hearts with terror or caution, but to free them. The theme is victory, not defeat.

The sacrament is thus a form of the Word, the Word in its proper sense as Gospel. It is not a new word or a different word, but *the Word*.[35]

People of God

The Church is the people of God. It goes by many names. It is organized in different ways. It lives in different climates and in different cultures, but it is one people.[140]

Preaching

The mission of the church. The purpose of the church is to preach the gospel to all nations. Jesus prayed for unity for His people in order that the world might believe. Fellowship is for the sake of mission. Those who preach reconciliation must themselves display the power of reconciliation.[54]

Trust

The creation of trust among the people of this Church is perhaps the most important single way to make our strength visible and effective. Trust is created by everyone being willing to listen, to grow in understanding, even to change our minds as we learn from one another how to work together.[152]

Unity

Christians have always believed that they were one people. It is part of their basic confession of faith: "I believe . . . in the holy Christian church." But never in history have they been able to fully manifest that oneness God has given to them.[117]

Universality

Thoughts while trying to get comfortable on an airplane. . . .

It is marvelous to meet Christians everywhere—in the heat, the cold, in the mountains and on the plains—poor, rich, shades of political opinion, tall, short, dark, light—the variety seems endless—but the faith is the same! How can any one church really believe that it can live alone or that it encompasses all truth? God has his people everywhere.[147]

The Gospel we confess is a universal Gospel. By this we mean that the Gospel is for all men. The gospel belongs to God, not to us. We hear it and respond by confession of guilt and thanksgiving for its free gift. We receive this gospel through preaching, through the sacraments of Baptism, and the Lord's Supper, through the witness of fellow Christians in word and deed, and by our own reading and listening to the Scriptures.

There is only one Gospel—just as there is one faith, one Baptism, one salvation. Wherever that Gospel of our Lord Jesus Christ is heard and confessed, the people of God comes into being. Lutherans believe that this does not happen only among Lutherans but in all Christian churches. It is our judgment that often this gospel is distorted, or incompletely understood or insufficiently confessed in some other churches and sometimes in our own. If there were no problems of this kind, there would be not many churches, but just one Christian Church.[112]

War and Peace

The issue of peace and war is primarily in the church's concern. Although it recognizes the necessity of the power of the sword for the state, and supports its proper use, the church thinks of the sword as only a last resort, valid only in the overcoming of evil and never as a means of pursuing ends which can be gained by any other means. The church does not seek to lord it over the state nor to substitute itself for the decisions of the state. It cannot interfere with the proper operation of the state—the use of reason for the good of all—but can caution the state to exercise its own prerogatives properly. In the present state of affairs in the world, it must advise caution, restraint, patience and even suffering rather than arms because war has become a more terrible weapon than ever before in human history. The church can recognize a purely secular state (even a Communist one) if that state through its own chosen methods recognizes justice without denying basic human rights. The church has no economic theory of its own, for example. The church can criticize a so-called free society if that society seeks aggrandizement of its own, becomes intolerant in its pursuit of its own good, or makes grave mistakes in judgment in the pursuit of justice.[41]

World

The church is the people of God in the world—a people organized into institutions in society. It is the gospel which creates the church and therefore its source is hidden. But the church lives consciously in the world and has the responsibility to engage in the fight for justice and the good of all. It recognizes the validity of the state and its powers and supports the state against anarchy. Thus the church cannot be silent or withdraw from the affairs of society. It trusts men to use their reason and interferes in the operation of society only in those instances when reason breaks down, evil becomes rampant, or its own freedom is threatened. Therefore it accepts the role of constructive criticism of the state in order to further the aims of the state but renounces the power of the sword for itself. The church also recognizes its own prejudice and sin and repents of them before the world.[41]

Mission

Adventure in Mission

Mission is the discovery of the possibilities of the gospel where you are. Mission is living by and for the gospel. Mission is what the church does. Mission is love in action. Mission is obedience to the Lord. Mission is the method of believing in the gospel.[125]

I invite you to join me in this high adventure of being servants of our Lord Jesus Christ for the time he has given us to work.[152]

I have *very* great hopes for the church. For if it can discover and do its mission, it will become a healing element in this society which I believe can come from no other source. It will become a catalyst as well as a conscience. It will become the rallying point for a new hope and for a new thrust forward in the life of this nation.[131]

We are a church in mission. We are a church which must think in terms of the task to be done.[132]

Celebration

So the most powerful gift that God gives man is the power of confidence, the power of faith, the power to trust, the power to overcome the depression and the limitations of life in the world with so much conflict and so much evil, and God expects us to utilize this power so that life for mankind becomes much better than it is when men refuse to take on themselves the responsibility for the good of all mankind.[140]

We truly believe in God, but often we act as though we did not. So it is not just a matter of articulating the gospel, having that warm, wonderful feeling of identity with the great community which believes that gospel and worships that Lord. It's also the question of the living out of that faith in such a way that this society sees that there are still those who live not only by themselves, but who live in the trust and the hope of God who has all of history in his grasp and leads it to his fulfillment.[132]

Nothing lifts the human spirit more, nothing gives life, a goal more than to share in a great cause.[133]

Change

Flexibility to respond to the need for changed structures is essential in a rapidly-changing society.[127]

I believe that we must continually be open to new paths. We should discover those particular tasks that we are to do in our time. The Church in America has now become a church in diaspora—a mission church. We are no longer the "establishment"—if we ever were. Our task is not too different from the Church in other lands across the seas. To discover this mission, to carry out this task of evangelism, to communicate the enthusiasm and the insights, and to implement the organizational forms to do this mission may be that priority which we have yet to articulate.[120]

I believe God is putting a great challenge in front of us. I cannot think of anything more exciting to contemplate. There are some good signs.[144]

Christianity and Culture

A church in mission is a church which lives by faith, and it is a church which lives in the world. And it is not surprised to find evil and sin, for it does not believe the world is an ideal place. It does not live by some kind of Utopian sense of what history ought to be. It lives in the history which is, and it aims to grapple with it.[131]

We should not become so identified with society about us that we cannot be critical of it, that we cannot be objective in our relationships, that we should not become so ingrown in the life of a single nation or of a single class or color of people or political party or values of a certain kind of economic system that we have lost the ability to stand over against that and say sometimes no.[140]

It's an interesting time in which to live. I shouldn't say that too often, but it's true.[132]

What has happened in the last hundred years of biblical research and theological discourse is that the gospel has been released from the cage of certain cultural and philosophical commitments and freed to stand alone. No universal creed of the church has been set aside. The confessions in our tradition have been held in higher esteem. Lonely voices have indeed cried out against particular claims of the faith. This has caused the academic theological community to think through the problem again and to correct corroded interpretations or stereotyped language. This will continue to happen as it has always happened. The gospel cannot be long tied to a particular world view, a narrow concept of the self, or a set of values culled out of a particular cultural history. It carries its own power and makes its own way.[63]

The mission of the church should bring us into direct contact with the intellectual and social forces in our total society. The church in the past was burdened with ethnic and geographical challenges which prescribed the task for that day. Having occupied the land from coast to coast and having passed from an emigrant generation to a native one, we need now to face the whole society as we find it. The church has been planted in the new world. Now it must live there. We must meet the thought forms, superstitions, ideological commitments and social distresses head on where they are and not only as they crop up within our ranks.[63]

Confession

I have confessed my faith many times in this Church and will continue to do so. To articulate the faith simply and clearly is the first priority for each of you. Until that faith becomes verbalized and shared, the love and the trust cannot be known and accepted.[152]

Congregation

Your congregation is where it really happens. We can get these divisions of the church to do this or that. When we tell them to do something they do it. You know that, don't you? They're scared of you up there in Minneapolis.[132]

The congregation is not a political arm but it can help train its people to be sensitive to its community and thus give good leadership to the quality of life of all. The congregation can be a catalyst for awakening a community to its needs and opportunities.[134]

Social action is not the mission of the church—it is the expression of a faithful church. It is a necessary outgrowth of the hearing of the gospel—it is not the gospel. We have yet to learn fully of the confidence God gives a faithful people. He has not placed all the burdens of his world on our shoulders. We are to live and act in a particular place and time with resources and gifts he gives. This means to me that the articulation of our mission for this time needs additional work and acceptance among us. And this means concentration on the life of the congregation. The nurture and coming alive of the people of God in their respective places ought to shape our concern and programs.[120]

Dialogue

It's extremely important that I listen, that I understand. It's important that I talk, that I argue, that I take another position occasionally to assist in the listening process. But you must never misunderstand that when I give an opinion that somehow that opinion in itself stands. It's only an opinion given to advance the conversation, to permit a situation to arise so that listening can take place in a better way.[132]

I want to listen.[132]

God's pilgrim church can discover new ways to live by and for the gospel. God opens up new avenues for service if we will listen and learn.[134]

Doing The Gospel

Awakening the Church to new life, to new mission, to a great effort to which we can all bend our efforts is surely a challenge of grand dimensions.[120]

The only question is, the only question is, how do you get the mission done? [140]

We have indicated that there can be no change in the first priority of proclaiming and acting out the gospel. That is what makes the Church the Church. We have no other reason for existence. But God may be leading us to "do" the gospel with particular emphases in our time. We must discover his leading.[120]

To be a Christian is to have a vocation, a vocation to live and proclaim the gospel.[108]

The mission of the church is as much a thrust, an expectation, a reality in the place where you live as it is in Hong Kong or Nigeria or India or New York City.[133]

For the gospel is something that is to be believed, to be proclaimed, to be lived, to be articulated, to be debated, to be criticized, to be analyzed, to be shown, to be defended, to be loved.[108]

Mission is really the purpose of the church. It is what the church does everywhere at all times. It is therefore what you do in your congregation, what you do in your life. The nurture and the renewal of the people of God where you are is its mission. And I'm not certain that everyone has this sense of mission, has this sense of urgency, really knows what it is the church should do.[116]

We are tempted to think we are really accomplishing our mission when we simply perpetuate ourselves.[120]

The theological task requires obedience to the gospel it seeks to interpret. There are many aspects of the task which are objective and neutral in character, but the main thrust of the work is devotional as well as intellectual. Acting out is as necessary as thinking through. The task is under the judgment of the gospel as well as a proclaimer of its good news. Those who do not confess and act out their faith are not proper performers of their responsibilities.[63]

To be a Christian is to have a vocation, a vocation to live and proclaim the gospel. That's a very important kind of sentence. To be is to have. That suggests that being a Christian is not something which changes one's nature. It does not make one into something different from what he was in his nature before. To be a Christian is not to become more than or less than a person. He does not become something other than what he was created to be, but to be a Christian is to have a vocation. It's to have a direction, it's to be placed into a context, it's to have a goal, it's to introduce moods. And this vocation, this calling, this direction can be defined as living and proclaiming the gospel.[108]

But I do raise a question as to whether we have fully understood our mission. We do, of course, do much mission work. The real question is, have we discussed together on the congregational level what our purpose for existence is and have we come to conclusions which have penetrated the whole life of the congregation and produced results in activities and commitments which reflect a solid faith? One way, perhaps, to get at the question in your place is to ask "What are we doing?" Does our doing reflect an interest only in perpetuating ourselves? Does our doing indicate that our only interest is in the future God has promised us? Does our doing show our love for all men around us and give us opportunity to enhance their life and hope?

Doing and believing belong together and ought to be consistent and clear in their relationships.[123]

If I live by the grace of God, and not by anything which I create in myself, then I am free. What is it that I should hang on to? What is it that I can lose? What is there that I must somehow grasp to my bosom as being mine if nothing in the end whatsoever is mine? It is all a gift from God. It is by this grace that we are made free. And if we then can be free, then we can serve. And we can serve with boldness, and we can serve with openness, and we can serve with readiness, and we can live in any age and any generation and face any task. That is the call of the gospel.[131]

Evangelism

We are sent people, and evangelism means going out, going out into the community, going out into the place where we work, going out into the whole world. If we can overcome these temptations of not just perpetuating ourselves, our customs, our particular ethnic group, our particular group of people of a certain class and type, and if we do not fall into the temptation of thinking only of heaven at some future time and can reorient ourselves as sent people, then we can really begin to do evangelism and can relate faith in mission[116]

Techniques are not in themselves evangelism.[116]

Evangelism is the name for a vocation of being and doing, of living and proclaiming the gospel.[108]

The abundance of manpower for the church is a blessing, not a problem, but we have to be more imaginative and active than we have been to utilize it properly.[129]

One can put it more crassly, and perhaps more bluntly, perhaps more meaningfully, to say there are two dimensions to the Christian life. One is to be a Christian. The other is to make Christians. It's a little dangerous to say it that way.[108]

Evangelism is a gospel word. It is not a law word.[154]

Evangelism means living by the gospel, proclaiming the gospel. The word itself comes from the Greek word which talks about the good news. The church lives and works and trusts and hopes in the gospel. Evangelism then becomes for me an overriding, integrating idea which unites that which the church believes and that which the church does. When the gospel is preached and believed and done, all kinds of good things happen.[116]

To be an evangelist means to have the evangel. The evangel is the name for gospel, the name for good news. Everybody is an evangelist. And evangelism is the expression, is the *exousia* of this grace in all dimensions of life. Not just in mass sessions with Billy Graham and evangelistic songs and things. Not just an emotional dimension of life which is of real and good. But in the very stance of life, in the way by which life has an imprint, in all that has the sacrificial aspects of life, the outgoingness of life, the choices of life, all of those things which relate to making the gospel something which is expressed in the life of persons.[141]

We Lutherans in America, I believe, are not smarter than other

Christians, but I believe we have something to contribute, some witness to give, and by the unity which we display among ourselves and the understanding of the gospel can become a powerful force for God in a mission in this society.[133]

To live and proclaim the gospel—I would say these two verbs, live and proclaim, can be brought together in one word. The word is evangelism. The word evangelism comes from the gospel, the word gospel. It really means to proclaim the gospel. So evangelism becomes the key word by which one understands the vocation of being a Christian.[108]

Fellowship

We believe that there has been an affirmation that we need to take deliberate steps toward fellowship. Fellowship will not grow without deliberate decisions by which we can impel each other toward fuller fellowship.[150]

Grace

Each of us lives each moment of each day by the grace of God, not by our own strength, not by our own will, not by our own intelligence, not by our advantages, not by that which we own, not that which is our goal, not our estimate of ourselves, but we live by the grace of God.[131]

The power of this gospel stills the fears of men, fears of meaninglessness and death, harnesses latent and active hostilities native to man's state of being, and inspires courage and hope. Love is engendered as its most perfect gift. In being freed from the ultimate consequences of his guilt and weaknesses, man is given the freedom to shape and direct his life as a new man, subject always to both failure and renewal, but always within the new circumstances of his changed state of existence.[63]

Justice

"Tell It Like It Is,"—these young people are reminding us what justice really is. It is God's freedom and his love expressed now.[140]

There is no reason why there should not always be complete openness in discussion and debate in the church and especially in legislative assemblies. Minorities should be heard. Dissent is proper. Clear procedures should be defined and followed. There should be no oppression and no "under the table" dealings. I think we are entering a new day and I rejoice in it.[139]

It is easy to become numb with the thousands of pictures of human tragedy that confront us on every hand. More people suffer today, in this modern affluent age, than in any time in the history of man. O, man's inhumanity to man! [123]

Leadership

A spiritual leader is not one who is autocratic, though sometimes firm, not one who permits all things, though he is willing to learn, but, like all others, a sinner saved by grace who trusts that God will guide through his Word.[152]

For me, Jesus Christ is the center of my life. I place myself before him as his servant above all allegiances. It is from this trust that I receive my strength, my firmness for those convictions for which I stand, my patience to listen and to wait, my understanding of my own weakness, and my hope for the future which he has not yet fully revealed.[152]

God does not need us. He does not need new curricula or old theologies. It would be difficult to say what he needs less, new revolutions or old establishments. God is in charge. He molds history in a direction of his choosing. He involved himself at the points in which he sees fit. He does not lean on us. If you think that you have a great talent that God desperately needs, forget it. If you think that your piety is ready-made to impress God, think again.[138]

My first priority is the faith of this Church and the life which ensues from it. The questions of morale and of direction and the dimensions of anxiety and hope are immeasurably more important than specific programs or organizations.[104]

I'm with you. I encourage you. I will work for and with you. Let's create a great team to do great work in a great church.[81]

This Church should be grateful when men or women give long and faithful service in these places, being assured that their work is subject to review and correction. The staff in the national offices need to understand that their work is not so much a profession as it is a calling and a service. They have no more rights to this particular work than any other servant of this Church. Rather their work is a privilege which this Church may change or discontinue. Sometimes it is the very zealousness for the cause by staff which is interpreted as offensive. I wish every servant in this Church were as devoted and competent as the national staff.[127]

I have on my desk, as some of you know, a little gift that was given me in San Antonio by a group of friends. It is a giraffe made out of nails, and it has a very long neck. And that's to remind me that sometimes I have to stick it out a long ways.[132]

> Being surprised by:
> the experience that district conventions vary considerably in their convention planning, program and participation . . .
> learning the reason my son was tardy 17 times this semester because he attended a prayer meeting before the opening of school each day!
> the marvelous lay leadership available in the church. . . .

the chagrined knowledge that National Secretary's
week was last week![139]
Have fun watching the flowers bloom![129]

The parish structure of the church is a sleeping giant. What army has ever had so many outposts, so many islands of strength, so many resources at its command? These forces are sometimes too dispersed, and the instructions confused and there is restlessness in the ranks but the strength of the Christian community should not be underestimated. The Christian community needs awakening, not abandonment.[63]

Love

I mean by the unalterable element the principle of *agape*. This is expressed in the language of law by Jesus in the command, "Thou shalt love one another," and as a summation of the law, "Thou shalt love the Lord thy God," and "Love thy neighbor as thyself." This is a paradoxical way of speaking. Love is law in the sense of being the ultimate necessity for the fulfillment of life, but it is not law in the sense of having a definable structure or being restrictive. Love is not a limiting principle, but rather a vivifying power. Both Paul and Luther struggled against "law" in order to maintain the power of the "new Law." Love makes unconditional demands, but it also is a power which breaks through all demands. Love is above law at the same time that it is law.[34]

People of God

If I were asked what were my chief concerns for the people of God today, I would have to answer first, the faith of the church, and second, the mission of the church.[116]

Most of our problems come in the way we relate to people.[140]

In the gospel you certainly do not find him apart from men, but he asked us to love and to serve those in whom he is.[150]

Every family on earth, says Paul, is related to God's name, and that means related to his power. Therefore, we respect every other man and find ourselves responsible to cooperate with all other men and learn from all other men because God has given the power of creaturehood to every man.[141]

We love one another, but we don't know how to show it.[141]

I should first of all like to thank you—to thank you for what each one of you does in the place from which you come. You lay people for the leadership you give in your particular place, for the support you give your pastor and the other leaders of your church, for the way you serve in your vocation, in your daily work, for your prayers and for your gifts.[133]

Preaching

Our real task for this day is to preach the gospel with such clarity, conviction, and power that a restless world will hear. God calls us to a task as great as that of the reformers. This is not a time to engage in the subtleties of theology but a time for firm proclamation and obedience to the love and grace he has promised us. How great is his grace![130]

Stewardship

We must do a better job of informing our people of what the money of the Church does.[120]

Structure

Structures in themselves don't mean very much, and they don't interest me very much. I just would like to have the best structures, whatever they might be, to get the job done.[140]

Unity

Inter-Confessional dialogs are probably the most effective means of improving relationships with other Christians.[120]

After several centuries of new divisions and schisms, Christians in our time have begun to work together, locally, nationally, and even internationally, in caring for the needs of the world. Councils of churches have been formed to assist in communication, study, and common work. This followed the New Testament example of the Council at Jerusalem which brought together Christians who were having a dispute in the time of Peter and Paul. World Conferences have been held to study the faith and attempt to reconcile differences, and to plan strategy in mission. Living room dialogues have helped lay people to discuss their faith with their neighbors.[117]

Find ways to relate to other Christian congregations. We cannot solve all the problems the various denominations have on the local level, but we can be friendly and cooperative with other churches so that a common witness and a common contribution can be made. It isn't always possible to find a friendly reception but let it never be said that we are the problem.[134]

The twentieth century will be known in future church history books as the beginning of the great effort to bring the Christian churches together again—as the search for understanding.[117]

We are members of the World Council of Churches. Although some of our people have difficulty understanding this membership, I believe that the great majority of our membership wishes to be related to the other Christian churches of the world.[120]

There is absolutely no doubt in my mind that the World Council is dominated by an evangelical spirit. The primary force which holds these churches together in this Council is the centrality of Jesus Christ. And if there are still deep divisions of understanding of the Christian faith, these differences in doctrine are all subservient to the confession that Jesus Christ is the Lord of all.[157]

I do not agree with everything that other Christians do, but I love them as brothers in Christ. I pray for the day when we can work more closely together and share in the gift of unity in him that our Lord gives us in his Holy Supper.

In the early church it was said of the Christians by the non-Christian world, "See, how they love one another." I hope that in our world of tensions, suspicions, and misunderstandings, it will also be said.

Pray, listen, and love one another! [112]

Universality

When you confess, "I believe in the holy Christian church," you confess that you are not just yourselves in this land, but you are a part of God's great movement in history.[140]

War and Peace

We are agreed that war is an evil which wreaks havoc on millions of people and brings devastation to the innocent as well as to the guilty. We agree that all of us share to some extent guilt for the hostilities among men, either intentionally or unintentionally. As Christians aware of our own sin and our own incapacities to deal with great questions with sufficient wisdom, we should never be hesitant to admit that guilt and repent.[120]

The Doctrine of the Church and Its Implications for Parish Education

I conceive of my task today in a way which adheres strictly to the title—to elucidate the doctrine of the church and to deduce from this whatever specific implications there may be for the teaching ministry of the church. This means that I do not come to you with any predelictions as to what the teaching ministry ought to be in terms of a particular philosophy of education or in light of any peculiar problems you may be facing in your staff work in a department of the church. If this topic is to have any value to you, it seems to me that it ought to approach the situation rather coldly and objectively, either giving theological undergirding to what is already being done or disturbing the presuppositions and principles by which you have been acting. I must confess that I do not know which it might do—I hope that it might do one or the other.

In fairness to you, I think it wise to suggest the presuppositions by which I operate, presuppositions which shape my understanding of the theological task and are to this extent the limiting factors in my concept of the church.

First, I accept the Lutheran Confessions as the prolegomena for theology; that is, I am a student before I am a teacher and I identify myself with that general orientation to the Christian faith provided me by the Reformation. I believe the confessions to be the correct exposition of God's message to man. This does not mean that I think of them as the only expositions of the gospel. There are other ways to express the gospel and I believe that traditions other than my own have valid interpretations which may have emphases or language variant from this historical expression, but it is my conviction that the Lutheran understanding is the most profound in Christendom. This is why I am a Lutheran. The basis of this conviction is that the confessions point to the Bible as the source and norm for their witness. The confessions are therefore always subject to scrutiny, criticism and even possible revision in light of the testimony of the only absolute standard. Theology I understand to be the continuing task of interpreting and fostering this dialogue between the Scriptures and the witness of the church in the Confessions. Theology therefore is always in process, finding new language, new patterns, new emphases. It is the language of the church as it seeks to proclaim the message of the gospel in any particular time or place.

Second, I consider the Material Principle to be the dominant principle in Lutheran theology. We have adopted the language of Formal and Material Principle—by formal principle meaning the definition of the character of our authority, the Bible, and by material principle, the message of that authority, in simplest terms, the good news that God, for Jesus' sake, forgives us our sins and makes us righteous. To put it bluntly, the primary aspect of the faith is not that the Bible is true, but that we are justified by grace through faith. The former is subject to the latter and not vice versa.

Third, the church is an integral part of the Material Principle. When the justification by faith concept is stated, the idea of the church is already anticipated. It is not a secondary or peripheral doctrine. It is not the last chapter in the dogmatics. It is not unnecessary or unimportant doctrine. It is, in fact, *the* doctrine. The whole

Christian faith could be exhibited in terms of the church—which, in fact, is what Luther himself did.

Fourth, the main hermeneutical principle is Christological. Everything in the Christian faith must be understood in light of its relationship to the Christ event. Everything either prepares us for Christ, is an exposition of his meaning or leads out from him. The Christian faith cannot be departmentalized into a series of unrelated subjects, but is rather of that character which radiates out from a common center. The metaphor is that of the rays of the sun, the single and energizing source, rather than that of a picture created by fitting together parts of a puzzle. The person and work of Christ is the central and determinative factor of the Christian faith.

Our first task is to ascertain the reality of the church. What is the church in itself? What is its being? The Reformation chose to capture this reality by using the New Testament word, *ecclesia,* denoting the community gathered by God through Christ, the community of believers, the people of God. The church is the people, the community of faith. As correct as this is, it must not be allowed to obscure the enormous variety of ways in which the New Testament expresses the church idea. There are more than 90 images in the New Testament, images such as: People of God, Israel, covenant community, body of Christ, members of Christ, in Christ, fellowship, kingdom, city, temple, priesthood, holy nation, household, family, sons, brothers, bride, vineyard, vine, tree, flock, saints, those elect, called, chosen, justified, sanctified, glorified, disciples, believers, the faithful, slaves, servants, stewards, ministers, witnesses, confessors, ambassadors, soldiers, friends, new humanity, new creation, body of righteousness, colony of heaven, exiles, pilgrims, those of the way, etc. etc. None of these is unimportant. The fluidity of thought and exuberance of imagination which they reveal is witness to the richness and mystery of the reality to which the names are given. We cannot hope to capture in a sentence that which the New Testament on its every page seeks to expose in this dazzling array of imagery.

We can, however, see patterns in this kaleidoscope. The patterns are best seen in what we can call the polarities of the nature of the church. The church, for example, is both human and divine. It is the people, people of flesh and blood, with sins and weaknesses and glories, a real sociological reality, living in history, in process, learning and forgetting, growing and receding, visible, in the world. But it is also divine, the body of Christ, in which Christ lives in this world, in which he acts. It is the arena of the Holy Spirit, the sanctifying agency, the entity which rises above history and participates in that quality of existence which is not confined by either temporal or spatial categories, invisible and hidden, not of this world. The church is both an end and a means to an end. God accomplishes in his church that which he has purposed and yet the consummation, the glorification, the end is not yet. He uses the church as the means by which he seeks to redeem the world and yet the church is that realm of redemption. The church is both being and becoming, both perfect and yet not perfect, both holy and sinful, both justified and yet not sanctified, both sanctified and yet in the process of sanctification. The church is a real community, perhaps the only real community of true inter-personal relationships, and yet is a divine reality, more than a community of men. It is completely unique in terms of the categories of this world. It is a mystery. The church is not the simple addition of individuals. It is more than this. It is a reality in itself. It exists before the individual and after him. He is incorporated into this reality through baptism, nourished in it through the preaching and the Lord's Supper. It is not faith of the individual which makes the church but by faith he lives in it. It is a living organism, created by God for his purposes, encompassing all history and yet peculiarly limited to time and place.

Realizing that the reality of the church cannot be fully encompassed, even though, as Luther suggested, it can be understood by a seven-year-old child, the Reformation sought to base its definition of the church upon the means which bring it into being. The church is the community of God *in which* the Gospel is taught according to a pure understanding of it and the sacraments are administered according to the Biblical Canon. The church is best known by its marks, by those forces which create it and sustain it, or as our tradition has it by the means of grace. Wherever the gospel is proclaimed, whether by formal preaching, or by individual witness, or by acts of love, or by celebration of the sacraments, there the church comes into being, for wherever the gospel is, there men respond.

The community is defined in terms of the relationship of Word and faith, or better, by grace and faith. These two must never be separated. Although the Word of God, the biblical witness, the historical events, have objective reality aside from men's faith, it is only by men's response that they accomplish their purpose, only where they both are, can the church be. Faith is a complex phenomenon but is chiefly defined as response to the redemption made known in the gospel. It includes acknowledgment of the truth of the gospel, obedience, trust, hope. It is the necessary means of receiving the salvation offered in the gospel. Faith is man's total response to the grace which is the gift of God. Faith must always be understood in relation to grace for it is the intersecting point of the sovereign working of God and the responsible action of man. The perspective of the New Testament is distorted when either element is minimized. The priority of grace, the divine action appears with special clarity in passages of the New Testament which link faith with the electing grace of God. The reality of man's responsibility appears with equal clarity in those passages which represent faith as obedience to the call of God, as well as in the inseparable interrelationship of repentance and faith. The role of Christ's redeeming act and that of faith are not of equal status but may be likened to source and vessel, gift and reception. (Some of this paragraph is paraphrased from *One Lord, One Baptism,* Augsburg Publishing House, 1961.)

It is at this point, I think, that we can draw our first implication for the teaching ministry of the church. We can call it the implication of necessity. The teaching of the gospel is integral to the nature of the church. It does not belong to the *bene esse,* that is to the well-being of the church, but to the *esse,* the very essence of it. If the church is the church, it is a teaching community. We can without apology consider the teaching ministry a ministry of grace, even a means of grace. The church can be properly defined in terms of its teaching. If the church does not teach, it is not the church. Teaching is therefore not an arm of the church, not an auxiliary function, not a secondary aspect of its life, but it is the church in action.

A number of secondary implications grow out of this basic principle. The church has no option about its teaching ministry. It cannot choose whether or not it wishes to teach. It teaches by the very virtue of its existence. How well it teaches is a measure of how well it is becoming the church. It follows as well that it cannot assign this function to anyone else—neither to the state or to an auxiliary agency, or even, I might add, even to the family, if in any way we consider the family to be a community separated from the fellowship of the church itself. And, of course, it means that the teaching ministry belongs to the whole life of the community. Not only in terms of the whole life span of the individuals in the community, from the moment of baptism on, but also to every aspect of the life of the community. The church teaches when the gospel is preached from the pulpit, when it witnesses to its faith in the sacraments, in the Christian conversation of its members, in its charitable acts, in its worship, etc. There is no time when the church is not teaching. If parish education defines itself as a responsibility to only part of this life, then it must understand that it is undertaking responsibility for only part of the teaching life.

The second main implication is that which we might call the implication of purpose, for the goal and nature of the teaching ministry is here defined. If the teaching ministry is a means of grace, then its purpose is man's response, that is, faith. I have searched for a word to capture the whole range of this idea. I don't know if there is one such word, but perhaps the idea fulfillment will do. The purpose of teaching is the *fulfillment* of faith. The many sidedness of this is breathtaking. It is to create faith where there is none, to revive it where it is lapsed, to strengthen it where it is faltering, to deepen it where it is shallow, to enlighten it where it is ignorant or mistaken, to make penitent the proud, joyful the discouraged, to increase faith for the immature, to reprimand the disobedient, to awaken the reluctant. Everything in teaching must focus at this point of accomplishing the goal of grace.

Thus we see that the two main implications of necessity and purpose grow out of the very fabric of the reality of the church, depend upon that reality and contribute to it.

We can explicate the character of the teaching ministry by examining the four time honored attributes of the church which we confess: the church is one, holy, catholic, and apostolic. I will have to confine myself to the specific ways they contribute to our understanding of our teaching task.

First, the church is one. It seems to me that this has implications for the *relevancy* of teaching. First, obviously, there is but one faith, one gospel, one church. The relevancy, that is, the integrity and effectiveness of this ministry must be measured in terms of how it contributes to the upbuilding of this *one* community. The relevancy of teaching is not best measured in terms of techniques, or even effectiveness of communication as much as in the accomplishment of the teaching. Everything must be measured against the answer to the question, does this contribute to the creation of the one new humanity, to the one true community, to the universal acknowledgment of the one Lord? I do not mean by this to advocate a so-called pan-protestant, or pan-Christian approach, but really quite the opposite, for it is my conviction that the best contribution to the unity of the church is to concentrate upon the communication of the one clear gospel, which I believe we have in our tradition. But this must be done in such a way that we do not create a sect, a loyalty to an institution, a narrowness which does not see the church in all its glory as Christendom. We must condemn error, for the sake of unity, but we cannot cultivate the feeling that because we confess to the one gospel, that all others do not have it in any measure. We have a difficult problem here because of the particular time in history in which God has placed us. Our task is not to create division but unity, our conviction is that it is the gospel that creates unity, a gospel proclaimed and lived in love.

A second aspect of this first attribute is the cultivation of the right correlation between the communal life and the individual. It is no secret that we have emphasized the role of the individual in his relationship to God so strongly that we have nearly lost the concept of the church. We must, however, not run the risk of committing the opposite error of losing the individual in some kind of mass emphasis upon the collective. The church is a real community. We have come to see that, in modern parlance, no man is an island and a self can be understood only in terms of its relationship to other selves. "*A* man is no man." But the new emphasis upon community and, therefore, the church, must not obscure the integrity of the self. A community is that relationship of selves in which the self becomes its true self. To say it in another way, it is in relationship to God that a man becomes that which God always intended him to be. True humanity can come to be only in dependence upon God, not in independency from him. This is saying at the same time that a Christian is one, who, in the life of his community, the church, becomes a true individual. He finds his freedom, his integrity, his "independence" within this frame of dependency, not only upon God, but upon his fellow believers. Communal life and individual integrity thus are in paradox.

Second, the church is holy, that is, the church is that place where the Holy Spirit is operative to make man holy and indeed does make them holy. The church is divine. This implies the *guarantee* of our teaching. Not anything we do can in itself make men respond. The guarantee is in the operation of the Spirit of God. We do not take upon our shoulders the whole of history and claim to be the gods who bring consummation to God's purposes. We are his instruments. His is the power. But we do not believe that we stand between God and man. In our teaching God is immediately present. In Baillie's words, the ministry of teaching is a "mediated immediacy." Where the gospel is, in act and witness, there the Holy Spirit is, doing the work of God. The real technique is his. To use a modern word, our teaching is a symbol, that is, with, and under our teaching the reality of God is communicated, not by virtue of the teaching, but by his wish and promise.

It is implied, further, that we are to teach the ways of holiness. Faith requires obedience, and we have the authority not only to relate the objective acts of God in which we are called to trust and by which we are saved, but to interpret this grace so that it becomes explicit in certain deeds, and attitudes in the whole of the routine of living. This does not mean that we are to create new laws, but are to teach the faith in such a way that obedience is required and obedience results.

There is the implication as well that growth is an integral part of the Christian life. The gospel is both simple and profound, both clear and mysterious, both narrow and broad. The leading of the Holy Spirit from simple to more profound understanding is not only characteristic of the communal life but implies a heavy responsibility to minister to every level of maturity at its own level with no cut off point.

Third: The church is catholic. The work of Christ is universal in character. It is for all men in all places in all situations. This implies the *context* of our teaching responsibilities. All boundaries of race, social status and even culture are eliminated. The church is a universal brotherhood. The context is therefore thoroughly human. It deals with the human problem of human interrelationships. Man's needs change. He is always in process, with new problems, new sins, new frustrations, new temptations. The teaching ministry is not only for the inner man, or the man in his personal life as the holiness of the church might imply, but it is for the man who meets the outer world as well, the man in the other communities of his existence, the state, the race, the social class, the job, the marriage relationship. Although the teaching ministry comes from within the community, it is for man in all his humanness, as he moves in this life in the historical context.

The work of curriculum building and revision is, therefore, never completed. There is always a new situation, a new medium of communication, a new vocabulary. It necessitates an interest by the educator in the object of his teaching, the student, in terms of his psychology, his world view and his particular problems in a particular time and place.

Fourth: The church is apostolic, that is, the church is bound to the norm of the apostolic witness. If we have felt that the foregoing implication opened the teaching ministry to vistas too wide to encompass, we are reminded again of the content of that which is taught. The static character of the message is explicit. The faith is bound to that event in history of the Christ, as witnessed to by the apostles and recorded for us in the Scriptures and handed down to us through the continuous community. We are the creatures of tradition. We turn again in the end to the act of confession. As others through the ages have confessed their faith in that one Christ, we join the mighty throng that marches through history clinging to that unique act of God in Christ. The objective character of teaching can never be lost. There is an inviolate obligation.

I think in this connection the special character of the sacrament of baptism should be mentioned. Both the human and the divine character of the teaching ministry is set in the larger context of what God has already done. The child, or the adult, should be taught in such a way that he understands that God has already acted on his behalf. The redemption was wrought on the cross. That redemption was given to me at my baptism. My whole life is a living out of the obligation occurred there. My faith is built upon the reality of that grace. My comfort stems from the fact that it is not my doing that accomplishes my salvation. Nothing can change the fact that I am baptized. God's grace of that moment stands like a tower that casts a shadow over the whole of life. Although I am continually being brought to faith and the goal of teaching to fulfill faith, that faith is set against the background of the primary act of God for me. We are involved here once again in the supreme paradox of divine sovereignty and human freedom. The Spirit is gained through faith and faith through the Spirit just as the grace of Christ follows on faith and yet conditions it as its basis. The content of faith is determined by the unchangeable reality of what God has done but it is appropriated and applied by my act of faith.

There are dangers in over-emphasizing the apostolicity of the church. We can center the attention so much on the historic character of the Christ event that we neglect a continuing interpretation of its meaning. We are always tempted to sentimentalize it. We need only to point to the effeminate heads of Christ which adorn our homes and the massive response to such gross misinterpretations of the Christ as the movie, "King of Kings." To preach the gospel on a teen-age level does not have to be the same as casting the life of Christ in the terms of the TIME review of "King of Kings," "I was a teen-age Jesus." It is all too easy in the elementary level to make a hero figure out of the Christ.

A second danger is to under-emphasize the apostolic character of the gospel by concentrating everything upon the intervention in life now. This moment becomes primary. Knowing God's will for this impatient time, expecting special revelations for this particular situation and other popular expectations among us dull or even obliterate the basic confession that God comes to us in the gospel and this gospel is in the historical category of the written Scriptures. We are neither Pentecostalists nor Quakers.

Confirmation must be seen in this light. Confirmation, simply put, is just what it says—a confirming of that which already exists. Whether or not confirmation is also preparation for first communion is a separate question. There is nothing in the nature of the church that demands either the rite of confirmation or first communion at a particular age. The community has the right to make decisions regarding its practices concerning this that seem good to it in light of the particular problems of its own age.

If in the foregoing, I have outlined the implication for the teaching ministry for parish education, in too grand and wide a manner, I can only say that I could do nothing else. If you had hoped for a neater and narrowed concept of your task, you have asked for the impossible. Your task is as great as the task of the church and must be conceived within the setting of this divine reality. The grandeur and the glory of the church is such that there is no end to the opportunities and responsibilities that those of us blessed by the gospel have but it also belongs to its glory that even a cup of cold water given in his name makes the angels sing, and the faith of a little child is the faith that can move mountains.

Acceptance Speech:

As president of Wartburg Seminary at the Omaha Convention, 1968

Twenty years ago I made a lonely and difficult decision. I was working, then, as a research chemical engineer for Standard Oil. I sat in my office high over the refinery with the smell of sulfur in my clothes and pondered a haunting call. I finally gathered my courage, took the night train to St. Paul and entered Luther Seminary to study for the ministry. I have never regretted that decision. Not for a moment. Theology has been for me the most fascinating, demanding and rewarding vocation I could imagine. It has been my privilege to be in succession a student, a pastor, and a teacher of theology. The call you gave me to teach theology has been for me the highest of vocations.

You in this convention have faced me with another difficult call. You have asked me to leave the work, the people, the place and the opportunities I love. I consider the gravity of my decision to be as great as that vocational decision of twenty one years ago. My answer has been reached only in these last days but is the result of much sober reflection. But the answer is clear and is based on two principles. My loyalty to the church as a whole must transcend my loyalty to any one institution in the church. My obedience to this call must supersede the call you gave me for my present work.

I am honored to be associated with the students, faculty, alumni, and destiny of Wartburg Seminary and I now identify with that new loyalty. And it is with firmness of purpose and calmness of spirit that I go, at your request, to a new life and responsibility.

The task you have given me is not easy. Theological education exhibits some of the turmoil that greets us on every side. I consider your call to me to be not only administrative but more primarily to engage in a struggle with three basic questions.

What is theological education? A seminary once had the image of a sleepy place, irrelevantly academic and certainly not revolutionary. But three new elements are now with us. The students you send us from your homes and congregations are lively, independent, and questioning. They reflect the environment you have given them and they demand more than we are able or prepared to give them in the present system of education. Their great compassion and open spirit must be channeled in new ways. There is an explosion of theological knowledge that needs keen minds and more diligent work than can be crammed into three years. And we now operate in an ecumenical context that requires new approaches and new responsibilities.

But this question cannot be answered without examining the question, What is the ministry? You laity have expectations of your pastor that go far beyond the pastoral image a generation ago. The new pastor must be skilled in pastoral work, in the dynamics of social concerns, in organizational prowess, in the handling of his own emotional stress in addition to sound theological competence. There are now a host of specialized ministries to be reckoned with and the ever increasing zeal and leadership of the laity to be considered. We must decide for what we are training a man.

But again, there is a more fundamental question facing us. In convention, we are considering a number of crises—as we should—but we haven't faced the crisis which underlies everything we do—

the crisis of the identity of the church: What *is* the church? We know how to define the church theologically. The church is the people of God. The church is the assembly of believers among whom the Gospel is preached and the sacraments administered. But we do not know how to translate this definition into our life in the world. The continuing debate about structures, the unresolved question about ministry, the role of the church in the world and the varying interpretations of the church in pre-convention report are all evidences that this supreme question confronts us.

These questions will be a continuing part of the responsibilities of the call you have given me.

I make two pledges to you as I go to my new work. First, I will keep ever before me the empowering force of the Gospel. The Lordship of Jesus Christ is for me the constant and renewing fact of my life. This means to me freedom from the errors and the limitations of the past and freedom to hope for and live for the future. I believe that the Lutheran confessions are the most cogent witness to that Gospel in Christendom and I shall seek to inspire love, confidence and zeal for these gifts God has given us in the Reformation.

And second, I pledge to give my every energy for the task. You ask for nothing less and I give it. By this I mean candor and honesty, disregard of ambition or favor, and the capacity to dream.

And I ask of you two pledges. In calling me, you have accepted a common responsibility. I ask, first, for your trust. I know that some of you are uncomfortable with some of the new problems in theology. I understand that. We should all be somewhat uncomfortable. But I am not afraid. The Gospel cannot be kept under a bushel. It must be examined in the light of day. There has hardly been a time in the history of the church, with perhaps the exception of the 16th century, when theology has been more exciting or the Gospel examined with more care. It *is* possible to be a modern man and an alive and confident Christian. The Pastor must be trained to serve not only you but also your children and your children's children. Trust us as we deal with 2,000 years of church history and the challenge of our time. The Gospel will prevail.

Second, I ask for your cooperation. If we engage in some new ways to train pastors, help us by giving us your interest, by sending us your best young men, by providing us with the staff and funds to do excellent work. The Seminary and the church must go together. Give us your good will and prayers. The Seminary is a servant of the church but also dependent upon the church.

I thank you for your confidence and I ask you for continued confidence. Together we can face the many tasks of today and the new uncharted ones of tomorrow.

Acceptance Speech:

AS PRESIDENT OF THE AMERICAN LUTHERAN CHURCH, 1970

Delivered to the General Convention of The American Lutheran Church upon his election as Supervising Bishop and President of The A. L. C. This speech was delivered Friday, October 23, 1970.

This is not the right time or the right place for me to say all that is on my heart, but there are some things I should like to share with you in a few moments so that you might know what is in my mind to some extent and you might get to know me that much better in this opportunity we have here in San Antonio.

Not many days before this convention opened, I came to a calmness of mind and peace of heart that I brought with me here. I was prepared to accept whatever might be the decision of this convention. I feel that calmness yet. I was helped in this by the faculty in my own seminary where we sat together one evening just a few days before we came. There are some wonderful people at Wartburg Seminary, and I want you to know that.

These kinds of things go through my mind. I think of you as a deliberative assembly who worked through to a decision yesterday in a way which I'm sure you feel, and certainly I feel, was one which did credit to a great body of people coming from diverse backgrounds with different levels of knowledge and different points of view about this decision. I thank you for the careful way in which you came to this call.

I think of you as people who represent congregations and districts of The American Lutheran Church in its wholeness. I think of congregations which are not here through your persons today—little congregations on the prairies that are struggling to exist, congregations in the midst of the city which are struggling with problems of our time, the more stable congregations in the middle-sized cities across our land, our congregations across the seas in the different mission fields—all the diversities both in style and spirit which are in the American Lutheran Church. I think of the congregation where I began my ministry, in a basement church in Our Saviour Lutheran Church, Staten Island, New York.

I think of Dr. Schiotz, the man whom I will succeed (although it's difficult for me to say that). I've known President Schiotz for many, many years. He was my counselor when I was a young student. He was once the pastor of my wife and her congregation in Brooklyn. He has been the man I have followed and known, and a man sometimes with whom I have had intense discussions in these many years. Do not expect of me what you have expected and received from him in these years of his great statesmanship.

I think of the other nominees. I'm not sure that you realize just what it meant to be one of the ten, for I have very deep respect for all of those men—some of them are my very good personal friends. And I think we had a mutuality about our respect for one another.

I want to speak a special word for the two men who were with me on that famous third ballot. David Preus was my colleague in my seminary days, and I have been close to him in the ministry ever since. He was my pastor for a time when I lived in Minneapolis, Minnesota. He and I exchanged good greetings of fellowship before this convention opened, and we did so as you heard again last night. I would have been happy to have followed him as president and he has said that also about your decision.

Dr. Belgum and I have known each other, too, for many years, but history has not placed us close enough together so that we have seen each other very frequently in these last years. But he and I too also greeted one another. He promised me his firm support. I invited him to come and talk with me about our mutual concerns in our common witness and he has agreed to do so.

I think of Wartburg Seminary, its students, its faculty, where I have been so very happy in these two years. I apologize, I think, in a sense, too, for pulling out the rug from under them in the sense of leaving them so quickly and in such a startling fashion. I thought about them very much last night when a group of students and faculty met in my hotel room.

I think of my family who have settled in Dubuque and love it there, and now must move again, although I think with interest and excitement.

I think of the Lutheran Church in America and the Lutheran Church–Missouri Synod, the two great sister churches that I have come to know very well in these years of my growing up, with a great many friends in those two churches. I pledge myself to work with them as closely as it is humanly possible, and by the guidance of God's Spirit to come to very much closer unity in the years ahead.

I think of Lutherans everywhere, the churches of the Lutheran World Federation. I think of Christians everywhere with whom we have close fraternal relationships.

And I think of others—of the depressed, of the suffering, of the disappointed, of the doubters, of those who are frustrated, those that in their youth are awakening to a world very different from what they had hoped it would be, and who are crying out for something more than we seem able to give them.

But most of all I think in these moments of our Christian faith which undergirds me and undergirds you. I am sustained by the faith that the gospel will remain the same. It was given once and for all, and it is still the living voice which speaks again and again to a changing world, a gospel which engenders hope, which casts out fear, which inspires love. There are many ways by which one can express that gospel and confess it. The New Testament is that sparkling jewel with its many, many facets, its many changes of language and perspective, the marvel of the multiplicity of the confessions of the gospel. But as a farm boy from Iowa named Kent Knutson, I turn back to what I learned in my confirmation in the explanation to the second article of the creed. I know of no more all-encompassing, more beautiful, more meaningful way for me to say what I believe: I believe that Jesus Christ, true God, begotten of the Father from all eternity, and also true man, born of the virgin Mary, is my Lord, who has redeemed me, a lost and condemned creature, bought and freed me from sin, death and the power of the devil, not with silver and gold, but with his holy precious blood and his innocent sufferings and death, in order that I might be his own, live under him in his kingdom, and serve him in everlasting righteousness, innocence, and blessedness, even as he lives and reigns throughout eternity.

I look forward to working for you, and with you in this day. For I think each one of you is a minister of this gospel, and you must find a role to play in your life by which you express this faith within the Christian community and in the world.

God does not promise us everything. He does not promise us wealth. He does not promise us the power to control history. He does not promise us worldly greatness. But he does promise us that he will give us grace to trust him, and this is the splendor of the church. There is the splendor. And I live and work in the light of that grace. I ask for your prayers. Thank you.

The Doctrine of Scripture

as taught in the American Lutheran Church

A Statement of Reassurance

A paper presented to Commission on Fellowship of The American Lutheran Church and The Lutheran Church–Missouri Synod by Dr. Kent S. Knutson, President of The American Lutheran Church, in March 1971. This is not an official paper of The American Lutheran Church, but a personal statement.

The purpose of this statement is to interpret the position of The American Lutheran Church concerning the Bible and its use and place in the life of the church.

The hope is that those who do not know or understand this commitment or who have raised questions concerning it may be led to see that The American Lutheran Church believes and teaches a view of the Scriptures which is taught by the Scriptures themselves and reaffirmed by The Lutheran Confessions and the history of the Lutheran Church.

This is done in the awareness that churches which have been separated from one another may have developed emphases or styles of speech which may differ at certain points but which nevertheless communicate the same faith and commitment.

I.

The American Lutheran Church believes that the Bible is the Word of God and is therefore the only infallible authority in all matters of faith and life. This written Word of God is at the center of the church's life, in preaching, in teaching, in witnessing, in worship and is applicable to all moral questions and decisions. The American Lutheran Church accepts and confesses the Lutheran Confessions as found in the Book of Concord and requires subscription to them of all its members, both congregations and individuals. This faith is clearly delineated in the constitution of the church as follows:

400. Confession of Faith

401. The American Lutheran Church accepts all the canonical books of the Old and New Testaments as a whole and in all their parts as the divinely inspired, revealed, and inerrant Word of God, and submits to this as the only infallible authority in all matters of faith and life.

402. As brief and true statements of the doctrines of the Word of God, the church accepts and confesses the following Symbols, subscription to which shall be required of all its members, both congregations and individuals:

402.1 The ancient ecumenical Creeds: the Apostolic, the Nicene, and the Athanasian;

402.2 The unaltered Augsburg Confession and Luther's Small Catechism.

403. As further elaboration of and in accord with these Lutheran Symbols, the Church also receives the other documents in the Book of Concord of 1580: The Apology, Luther's Large Catechism, the Smalcald Articles, and the Formula of Concord; and recognizes them as normative for its theology.

404. The American Lutheran Church accepts without reservation the symbolical books of the evangelical Lutheran Church, not insofar as but because they are the presentation and explanation of the pure doctrine of the Word of God and a summary of the faith of the evangelical Lutheran Church.

The source and further explication of this understanding is found in the United Testimony of Faith and Life which was approved by the uniting churches of The American Lutheran Church in 1952 and reaffirmed by the Third Convention of The American Lutheran Church in 1966. Because The American Lutheran Church believes that Word and Sacrament should not be separated in the life of the church, the statement is headed "The Means of Grace" and follows in full.

The Means of Grace

God has willed that the knowledge and benefit of Christ's redemption be brought to man through his Means of Grace, namely, through the Gospel in the Word and in the Sacraments. Through these Means of Grace he not only offers, but actually bestows, his grace in Christ unto forgiveness of sins and a life of everlasting fellowship with him.

THE WORD

We believe that the Holy Scriptures of the Old and New Testaments are the Word of God, given by inspiration of the Holy Spirit for the purpose of man's salvation. Through the Scriptures the Holy Spirit informs and convinces us that his Word is true, that he will keep all his promises to us, and testifies in our hearts that our faith in Christ is not in vain. "Sanctify them through thy truth: thy word is truth" (John 17:17, AV).

We bear witness that the Bible is our only authentic and infallible source of God's revelation to us and all men, and that it is the only inerrant and completely adequate source and norm of Christian doctrine and life. We hold that the Bible, as a whole and in all its parts, is the Word of God under all circumstances regardless of man's attitude toward it. "All Scripture is given by inspiration of God, and is profitable for doctrine, for reproof, for correction, for instruction in righteousness: that the man of God may be perfect, thoroughly furnished unto all good works" (2 Tim. 3:16-17, AV). The Bible is the Word of God, given by inspiration of the Holy Spirit through human personalities in the course of human history. "For the prophecy came not in old time by the will of man; but holy men of God spake as they were moved by the Holy Ghost" (2 Peter 1:21, AV). We acknowledge with humble gratitude the condescending love of God in speaking to men through the agency of human language. We reject all rationalizing processes which would explain away either the divine or the human factor in the Bible.

The Holy Scriptures contains both Law and Gospel, but the primary content of the Holy Scripture is the Gospel. The Law is brought into the service of the Gospel by working in man a realization of his sinfulness and of his need of redemption, by awakening in him the terrors of conscience since he stands under the wrath of God, and by revealing to him God's holy will. The Gospel brings to the penitent sinner the assurance of God's pardon and the promise of victory over sin.

We hold it basic to the right use of the Bible as the authoritative revelation of God to man that it must be its own interpreter. All interpretation of Scripture must be in the light of Scripture itself with its central theme: God's loving purpose to save men in Christ.

The Sacraments

In and with his Word Christ has instituted for his church two Sacraments: Baptism and the Lord's Supper, which bear his seal and promise.

Baptism. In the Sacrament of Baptism, which is the "washing of regeneration and renewing of the Holy Ghost," we are born again of water and the Spirit, receiving the Holy Ghost and the forgiveness of sin, and are made members of Christ's body and citizens of his kingdom. In receiving Baptism we are made partakers of Christ's death and resurrection.

We believe that it is Christ's will and command that infants be baptized and that they be nurtured and instructed in the Christian faith. Such Baptism is the establishment of the covenant of grace, which has everlasting validity unless it is rejected in unbelief, and it is a clear proclamation of the Gospel of grace for all men.

When Baptism is administered later in life, as a Sacrament and Means of Grace, it admits the baptized person into fellowship with Christ and his church and through faith assures the believer of his full status as a child of God.

The benefits of Baptism are not dependent upon the mode in which the water is administered but only upon the word and promise of Christ.

The Lord's Supper. In the Lord's Supper Christ gives us his body offered up for us and his blood shed for us, to eat and to drink for the forgiveness of sins, the strengthening of our faith, and the increase in holiness of life. "The cup of blessing which we bless, is it not the communion of the blood of Christ?" The bread we break, is it not the communion of the body of Christ?" (1 Cor. 10:16 AV).

By virtue of Christ's promise we hold that all communicants receive the body and blood of him who is present not only in the congregation observing the Sacrament but in the Sacrament itself. Faith in Christ as the Savior from sin, and faith in his promise in the words of institution, together with repentance, are necessary for a worthy participation in this Sacrament. The church therefore has the duty to withhold this Sacrament from openly ungodly and unbelieving sinners, since Christ's promise of forgiveness is rejected by them. Faith does not make or unmake the Sacrament, but is required for the salutary use of the Sacrament.

We believe that we receive Christ's body and blood in Holy Communion, and the basis of this faith is our Lord's promise and assurance, not an ability conferred on a priest to change bread and wine into the Lord's body and blood by reciting the words of institution, nor the intention of a congregation to partake of the body and blood of the Savior. The Lord is personally present during the celebration of the Holy Communion to give sacramentally what he promises in his Word.

Because The American Lutheran Church realized that questions were raised by some concerning the fidelity of the handling of this commitment in the schools and congregations of the church, the Third General Convention adopted a further statement which sought to explain our policy concerning these matters. The statement follows:

In mutual concern for the mission of the church and in response to questions over some teaching and over some preaching in the church, the following statements were made:

1. The American Lutheran Church encourages intensive and honest scholarship in all areas of knowledge relating to the faith. It acknowledges as its duty, under God, to speak to each generation with the fullest possible consideration of the alternatives which threaten to distort or deny the faith once delivered to the saints. It is committed to avoid all rationalizing which would explain away the divine or the human factors which the Holy Spirit has used in revealing God's will for mankind.

2. Responsible stewardship of the Gospel demands that our teachers and pastors regard seriously the concepts and language which have been in traditional use in the life of the church, and that they

avoid the offense which may be caused by language which creates confusion and doubt over against the declared faith of the church. When new forms of language are used, care must be exercised that the great truths of the church's confessions be not undermined.

3. The American Lutheran Church adheres firmly to the principle that every interpretation of Scripture must be in accord with Scripture, and rejoices therefore in the earnest and painstaking efforts that are being pursued by its teachers and pastors to determine precisely what God is saying to his people in the Bible.

4. The American Lutheran Church declares that to determine what is distinctly Lutheran in the teachings of the church, the norm must be the confessions or symbols which for centuries have been definitive for the Lutheran family. To contend or imply that to be a Lutheran one must subscribe to something more or less than the confessions themselves, is to demand something other of a teacher or a pastor than is required by the Constitution of the church.

5. The American Lutheran Church believes that the Holy Spirit does not abandon the church. He inspires its search for truth and he strengthens its members in their love of one another. Within the great unity that they all have in Christ as Lord and Savior, he tolerates and even encourages a plurality of emphases which indeed adds to the riches of the church's life. It is in this confidence of the Holy Spirit that the church prays for an increase of both love of the brother and unity in the faith.

In the light of these affirmations we add the following observations:

A. Knowing that the devil is pleased to have the church dislodged from the pure teaching of the Gospel, The American Lutheran Church urges upon its pastors and teachers the utmost vigilance that God's Word be taught and proclaimed in such a way that souls are brought to the conviction of sin, to repentance, to the joy of forgiveness, and to the new obedience which is in Christ.

B. The American Lutheran Church deplores the confusion that is created by the disdainful use of such terms as orthodoxy, neo-orthodoxy, the new theology, liberalism, rationalism, pietism, fundamentalism, modernism, and believes that the church will best be served if pastors and teachers avoid using any label in their mutual search for the message of Scripture and in speaking of one another's efforts.

C. Although redeemed and restored to fellowship with God through Jesus Christ, the believer still lives in the limitations of the Old Adam. His sanctification never achieves perfection in this life. His will cannot attain perfect holiness nor can his mind attain perfect knowledge. His best efforts to formulate a theology in terms of propositions and statements will fall short. To assume that the church can arrive at human concepts or expressions that are in every respect complete* is as much a symptom of pride as to assume that the church or its members can achieve sinlessness in their daily lives. Both in living the faith and in knowing or expressing the faith, we all need daily forgiveness and amendment which the Holy Spirit alone can give. (*Amended by the Church Council, June 1970, to read "complete" rather than "correct" which had been a source of misunderstanding.)

D. The American Lutheran Church is grateful for the vigor of theological endeavor among its teachers and also for the responding concern for theological integrity among its pastors and people. Let no one hold a brother in disdain, nor charge him with either obstinacy or unfaithfulness without first exploring in love a basis for understanding. Mutual trust is a priceless treasure and is basic to genuine fellowship in the church. If brothers who differ or who seem to differ in theological expression will in charity "put the best construction" on what is said and done, the church will grow together in the life which we all share in Christ Jesus, our Lord and sound, historical, biblical doctrine will be affirmed among us.

II.

Some personal comments on the significance of this commitment might be helpful.

1. The phrase "Word of God" is dear to all Lutherans and a key to our understanding of God's disposition toward sinful man. The phrase has many implications and dimensions which are broader than its application to the Bible as a book. We use "Word of God" as the Bible itself does, that is, to mean God's power of creation, his communication to his people in the past, the redemptive events by which he revealed himself and the person of Jesus Christ who is the "Word become flesh." We use "Word of God" to refer to contemporary acts such as the preaching of the Word of God, the ministry of the Word of God and the sacraments.

In this paper we identify the Scriptures as the Word of God for they are written interpretation and communication of the Word revealed in the past in God's many actions and especially in his Son, Jesus Christ, and so are also the Word of God in themselves.

We also use "Word of God" to refer to kinds of Word within the Scripture. These are summarized in the phrase "Law and Gospel." God's Word is sometimes a harsh word, a word of wrath, by which he judges and condemns. We agree with Luther who called the Gospel God's proper Word, the Word which saves and redeems us. To properly understand the Scripture, we must understand it as both Law and Gospel.

In these various usages, it is always presupposed that God caused the Scriptures to be in His own way. He empowers them with His Spirit and He means for them to have the purpose of salvation.

The Scriptures are the Word of God in an objective sense, that is, they are God's Word for us even if we do not believe them. But, in another sense, it is proper to say, with Luther, that they also become the Word to us when we respond in faith, that is, they accomplish their purpose of the proclamation of the Gospel when they are heard.

The Bible, therefore, is what God wants it to be. We discover what His Word to us is by studying and listening to this book. We cannot make the book into something we would like it to be. We must be subject to it and must accept whatever we discover about it as we continue to learn from it. We must be open to new insights, to new knowledge about its origins or particular historical backgrounds as we unearth new aspects of its rich and miraculous history.

2. Perhaps the most important word that is used to describe the Bible is authority. We speak freely and confidently of the authority of the Word of God. The word authority is a translation of a Greek word which can also be translated power in English. The Bible is authoritative because God's power is manifested in and through it. Its authority is part of its nature. Man does not establish its authority by using particular words to describe it, proving it, or devising other human methods to ascertain its validity. Its authority is best understood by listening to it and obeying it. To the man of faith the Bible is the supreme authority for both this life and his everlasting salvation. Those who preach and teach in the church must have certitude regarding this authority so that they preach and teach with power, a power given to them by the Holy Spirit himself.

This authority is not diminished by the fact that God has chosen to reveal himself through human history and human beings. God has chosen to use means to reveal himself. God comes to us through words in a book which men have translated, interpreted and printed in their publishing houses. He comes to us through the water of baptism and the bread and wine of the Holy Supper. The divine word is never separated from the human means through which God reveals himself. Even his supreme gift, His Son, Jesus Christ, is a true human being in whom the fullness of God came to dwell. He is both God and man.

3. The use of the word *inerrant* in relation to the Scriptures has been much discussed. Because it is a word not used in the Scriptures themselves, it is subject to analysis and debate. Like all other words, it can be used both properly and improperly. When properly used, it communicates the faith that the Bible is true and can be trusted. God does not lie. His message of salvation is both perfect and sufficient. When improperly used, the term communicates the view that faith is required *because* the Bible can be proven to be historically accurate. This kind of "intellectualizing" of the faith is harmful to a true understanding of faith as a gift of God's grace.

Scholars who use the word do so with great care, taking these matters into account. (See the article by Dr. Robert Preus, "Notes on the Inerrancy of Scripture," Concordia Theological Monthly, June 1967, p. 363 ff.) Scholars who warn of its uncritical use, do so with the purpose of clarifying a right attitude towards Scripture so that Scripture may remain what it is without human attempts to force it into an artificial perfection. (See the article by Dr. A. C. Piepkorn, "What Does Inerrancy Mean?", Concordia Theological Monthly, September 1965, pp. 577-593.)

The American Lutheran Church uses the word inerrancy without hesitation in referring to the Word of God but does not require its use as the only or the best word to communicate the truth of

Scripture. Some in The American Lutheran Church prefer the word infallible to characterize the Bible as God's never failing promise of salvation. This avoids being misled by such questions as "Does the word inerrant require us to question the truth of Scripture when quotations vary, or adopt the world view of a biblical writer as an accurate description of the world as we experience it?" or "Should we distrust Scripture because our most ancient manuscripts vary from one another in some details?"

Whichever word is used, we do not believe that faith in the Word is undercut or that our commitment to the truth of Scripture is reduced. The word inerrant is certainly widely used in our church as a way to establish one's faith in the truthfulness of his Scriptural witness.

4. The word *inspiration* is emphatically affirmed in The American Lutheran Church as the proper word (in the light of II Tim. 3:16) to define the faith that God speaks in the Scripture. The Scripture is "God-breathed," that is, God's life and message are communicated in the Scripture. The phrase "verbal inspiration" is proper because it attests that it is through these words themselves that God speaks. This is why we put so much emphasis upon biblical exegesis and require our theological students to learn the Greek language and the methods by which the true understanding of the words can be ascertained. The word inspiration is sometimes confused with inerrancy as though God requires a particular kind of word in order to speak his truth. We believe that God speaks in the Bible in various kinds of language. He speaks even though there may be a problem in establishing the relation of a particular text to the historical event connected with it because we lack information. God is more interested in our salvation than our curiosity. Other terms, such as "plenary inspiration" (fully inspired) or "personal inspiration" (God speaks through the persons of the biblical

writers) are also useful terms. No one term completely communicates the fullness of the mystery of God's revelation.

5. The proper use of the so-called "historical criticism" has caused some concern, to us as well as to others. The term "historical criticism" is not always clearly understood. It is a technical term and does not imply criticism in the popular use of the word. It means rather a critical analysis of the Scripture from all perspectives in order to ascertain the fullness of the Scriptural message. The Bible is a book of history. The most elementary approach to the Bible, even the simple reading of it, must take into account the background and context of the words being spoken. Historical criticism may be improperly used as a scholarly method, as indeed can all other kinds of approaches to the Bible, but it also holds great promise for discovering insights and clarity in dealing with difficult passages in the Bible. The control in this activity remains the position taken in the Lutheran Confessions which submit themselves to scrutiny in light of the Scriptures.

6. Some have argued that there is a kind of reductionism in theology today. This has occurred because some scholars are radically skeptical of biblical history or speak of the Gospel in such a vague and subjective way as to discount the "sola scriptura" principle which requires fidelity to the whole of Scripture. The American Lutheran Church rejects the historical criticism which reduces the Scripture to a record of ideas without historical base or which denies the faith clearly confessed in the Bible and the Confessions. As an example, although we cannot penetrate fully the profound mystery of the resurrection of our Lord, or completely reconstruct all details of the history of those tumultuous days of his passion, we consider a denial of the historical resurrection of Jesus as a distortion of the faith and this clearly outside the limits of an acceptable theological position.

We also clearly affirm both the formal and material principles in Lutheran theology, that is, the whole Bible is our authority and that the Gospel, the message of the all-sufficient redeeming grace of our Lord Jesus Christ, is the message of Scripture. In this affirmation, we believe these two principles are inter-dependent. Neither can be denied. At the same time, it is the singular purpose of Scripture to awaken faith in the risen Lord Jesus Christ. We understand this to be the emphasis of our Reformation heritage when it speaks of "Word Alone," "Faith Alone," and "Grace Alone."

7. The American Lutheran Church has adopted a position of openness with regard to the discussion of theological questions in the church. Some questions have been under debate in the churches for centuries and some are new to our time brought to light by intensive study of the Scriptures. We believe that proper discussion of these issues in the open enhances the Gospel and we trust in the work of the Holy Spirit to guide us in these continuing discussions. Nothing has led us to change our full commitment to the Lutheran Confessions or to our faith that the Bible is true and carries out God's intent to reveal himself to us and to save us. During these discussions, some person may advance an opinion which seems to others to be wrong or to distort this understanding. This situation is handled by further discussion in a pastoral manner until the matter is resolved. No pastor or teacher in The American Lutheran Church may persist in a denial of the teaching of Scripture or the Lutheran Confessions. It is possible that some disagreement in a certain matter may continue within the framework of the commitment to the truth of Scripture and the Confessions as has always been the case in the church. We together seek for further wisdom and clarity regarding God's will as we continue to learn from the Scriptures.

The attitude of no single person should be interpreted as the understanding of the whole church. Incidents occur in all churches which cause temporary misunderstanding.

Other churches may adopt other stances in regard to theological discussion. About this we have neither comment nor criticism but we do not believe our policy either harms the fidelity of the church's faith or is divisive of altar and pulpit fellowship. Rather we believe that our life as a church has benefited from this great desire to examine the Scripture with full openness and freedom.

* * *

The American Lutheran Church rejoices that its discussions with the Lutheran Church–Missouri Synod have resulted in a memorandum of understanding such as "The Lutheran Confessions and Sola Scriptura" and that the further discussions among the theological faculties, which explored all these questions, has resulted in the agreement that we use and understand the Scripture in the same way in our churches.

This has been a brief statement which has been prepared so that people not acquainted with some of the more technical language employed in theological discussion may understand. It has not been possible to explore all the aspects of our rich heritage. One must add, too, that it is quite possible to misunderstand or to distort any sentence or paragraph in this paper. Each sentence must be understood in the context of the entire view. It has sometimes been the case that theological positions such as this have been grossly misinterpreted by isolating sentences or phrases or by being unwilling to seek for the intent of the author.

Theological discussion will continue within our churches as well as between them. We do not believe that the problems which confront us in preaching the Gospel in this age are greatly different in our churches. We believe that we should approach them together in the spirit of acceptance and humility, trusting that God will guide it with His Spirit to remain faithful to his Gospel.

Convention Address:

to the Lutheran Church – Missouri Synod Milwaukee, 1971

My dear brothers and sisters in Christ Jesus our Lord,

I come as a friend to speak to friends. And I come with joy in my heart to bring you greetings from the congregations of The American Lutheran Church. At our 1968 convention a resolution was presented to declare fellowship with the Lutheran Church–Missouri Synod. That resolution was many years in coming. Decades of prayer and preparation, several years of consultations in the churches which preceded the formation of The American Lutheran Church, and several years of consultation with you by the present American Lutheran Church. We were ready. The vote was completely unanimous. Because we deal with fellowship questions very carefully this resolution was submitted to a referendum to every congregation, and the vote was nearly 100% voting yes. There were no conditions, no hesitancy, just joy and a trust that this was God's will. So I greet you from every congregation of The American Lutheran Church in the words of Paul's letter to the Ephesians: "Let us give thanks to the God and Father of our Lord Jesus Christ, for he has blessed us in our union by giving us every spiritual gift in the heavenly world. Before the world was made God had already chosen us to be his in Christ so that we would be holy and without fault before him. Because of his love God had already decided that through Jesus Christ he would bring us to himself as his sons. This was his pleasure and his purpose. Let us praise God for his glorious grace, for the free gift he gave using his dear Son, for by the death of Christ we are set free and our sins are forgiven. How great is the grace of God which he gave to us in such large measure."

We know of course that your history with this question has been different and that some of you still struggle with this new situation of fellowship. We seek to be understanding. We struggled for many years too. We hope that you will be made free from your doubts and may rejoice with us. My own heart yearns for all of you to share our joy.

I was weaned on Walther's *Law and Gospel,* taught by the same teacher in the same classroom as your president. I have studied your great writings, especially the *Christian Dogmatics* of Franz Pieper, and have come to know many, many of you so well that I feel very much at home in your company. You are the people of God who have received his great grace. I belong to Christ, and in union with him I also belong to you. For so great is his grace.

I come as a grateful servant to thank you for your great work. We thank you for your proclamation of the gospel in this land and throughout the world. We consider you to be a great church, not because you are wealthy, not because God has given you greater wisdom than others, not because your leadership as a church in many areas of church life, but because you are faithful to the gospel. That alone is your greatness. And that is a gift from God and not of your own making.

The American Lutheran Church is a great church too, not because it makes any claims to wisdom, not because it is many or energetic in its tasks, but because it lays hold on God's grace and is faithful. How great is his grace.

I come as a seeker to listen so that I may get to know you better.

We need to listen to each other so that we may understand the many areas of life today, and we need also to listen to one another in the churches. I grew up on a farm in central Iowa and was taught the faith I still hold in a little white country church. How often I have thanked God for that faith! But we were isolated in many ways from you. There were caricatures of you among us. I was told then that you were cold and callous, too intellectual in your approach to the faith, and that you did many wicked things, such as drinking beer. We were so self-righteous. We thought only we were evangelical. But I have learned that we were wrong, when I grew up and met some of you and got to know you and could make my own judgments. We as an American Lutheran Church have matured, and now we know that you are an evangelical church, as warm in your love for the Lord as we, perhaps unsurpassed among all the people of God. I suppose that there are caricatures among you about us. How could it be otherwise, since many of you do not know us except through the interpretation of others. I hope that you will listen to us, to hear what we are really saying and how we really are.

As I listen to you, I hear some questions. Let me speak to three of them; my momentst are short, and I must be very brief.

I hear you asking about the attitude we have toward the Lutheran Confessions. I can tell you that I have studied these 636 pages of the Lutheran Confessions with great care, and you laymen perhaps for the first time should see what that book really looks like. They have been the basis of all my teaching for more than a decade as a theological professor, for I believe that in the sixteenth century God chose a man to speak the gospel in such clear and unmistakable terms that the whole course of Western history was changed. These confessions are the articulation of that gospel of the Scriptures, and I believe them to be unparalleled in Christian history. They are the identity of the Lutheran tradition. They are my witness, my theology, and the faith by which I live, for they are the true exposition of the word of God. They are true and they are sufficient. Anyone who has heard me speak to pastors, to lay institutes, to the national staff of The American Lutheran Church, to the many district conventions this spring, knows that I emphasize again and again the decisive role that these confessions must play in our life.

I hear you asking about our understanding of the Bible. Some of the things I hear you say sound strange to my ears. You must surely be speaking about another church or another person. It is possible in all innocence to take an isolated sentence in a lecture or a book somewhere and so interpret it as to distort the intent of the author. Listen now to what you hear and make your own judgment. From our constitution: "The American Lutheran Church accepts all the canonical books of the Old and New Testaments as a whole and in all their parts as the divinely inspired, revealed, and inerrant word of God and submits it to this, and submits to this as the only infallible authority in all matters of faith and life." Put that against your own constitution. Or listen to the United Testimony on Faith and Life, which was the basis of the formation of The American Lutheran Church. "We believe that the holy scriptures of the Old and New Testaments are the word of God, given by inspiration of the Holy Spirit for the purpose of man's salvation. Through the scriptures the Holy Spirit informs and convinces us that his word is true, that he will keep all his promises to us and testifies in our hearts that our faith in Christ is not in vain." Or listen to my own words: "The Bible is the word of God and is therefore the only infallible authority in all matters of faith and life. This written word is at the center of the church's life, in preaching and teaching, in witnessing and worship, and is applicable to all moral questions and decisions. The scriptures are the word of God, for they are the written interpretation and communication of the word revealed in the past in God's many actions, and especially in his Son, Jesus Christ, and so are also the Word of God in themselves. God caused the scriptures to be in his own way. He empowers them with his Spirit, and he means for them to have the purpose of salvation. The scriptures are the word of God in an objective sense; that is, they are God's word for us even if we do not believe them. In another sense it is proper to say, with Luther, that they also become the Word to us when we respond in faith; that is, they accomplish their purpose of the proclamation of the gospel when they are heard. The Bible is what God wants it to be. We discover what his word is to us by studying and listening to his book. We cannot make the book into something we would like it to be. We must be subject to it and must accept whatever we discover about it as we continue to learn from it." We could go on to discuss authority, inspiration, inerrancy, infallibility, law and gospel, formal and material principles, and many of the great used in our tradition, and we could do it in Latin or German, or your president and I could do it in Norwegian. I have submitted a short paper dealing with these matters to President Preus, and it is available to you. The Bible is the word of God. That is our faith.

I have been asking questions, I have been hearing you ask questions about the ordination of women. It is a troublesome question for us, for you, and for many others. Let me try to sketch our history of it and our attitude toward it. Many of our sister churches in Europe have debated this issue for many years. Sometimes there has been much bitterness. In every case after years of discussion they have decided to admit women to the ministry. The American Lutheran Church did not wish to act alone on this matter or to incur the same kind of bitterness. It was The American Lutheran Church, therefore, which asked the Lutheran Council to study this matter as objectively as possible. We wanted your representatives to be involved. We did not know what the outcome of the study would be. You have had your representatives involved every step of the way. Your representatives on the special subcommittee helped to prepare the document, which did not recommend ordination but said that each church in its freedom could make this decision within the freedom granted by the scripture and without being divisive of fellowship. One of your representatives did object. Your representative was chairman of the Division of Theological Studies at that time. The three presidents of that time sent the study to the churches for their reaction. Many forums were held throughout this country. Many of your people told us that although your church might make a different decision that it would not be divisive of fellowship. Others were very troubled by it. Your president did tell us at San Antonio that it would be troublesome if we should take this step. Our delegates listened to all the evidence and to the many different voices and on that basis made a decision. And as a free and sovereign church they made their own decision. They did so out of the conviction that this was not contrary to the scriptures when all the evidence was considered, and they did it believing that it was not divisive of fellowship. They believed, I think, that the Bible is not a book of laws, and the many admonitions to the church in the Old and the New Testament must be carefully delineated to understand their impact and application to the life of the church at other times and places. You are a free and sovereign church. You, as I understand it, have made your decision. We will not be offended if you take a different decision on this matter, if you did so based on your conviction of what the scripture teaches, but we would indeed be sorrowful if you did by this action make difficult or break our fellowship. The American Lutheran Church can err. The Lutheran Church–Missouri Synod can err. What shall we do when we both act out of our conviction that this is what the Bible allows and teaches? This is what we do—we live together and we seek greater wisdom. Let us not act hastily in judging one another without listening to one another. We believe God's grace is great enough to us, is great enough for us to live together in the freedom he has granted us.

I come as an evangelist to urge you to the great mission of the church. Our real task for this day is to preach the gospel with such clarity, conviction and power that a restless world will hear. We live in a troubled time, a time of massive dislocation, of social justice, a time of distorted sexuality, a time of growing secularization, which is another name for a growing atheism. God calls us to a task as great as that of the reformers. This is not a time to engage in all of the subtleties of theology, but a time of firm proclamation and obedience to the love and the grace he has promised us. How great is that grace!

I come to you as a sinner to testify to his saving grace. This is what we all are—sinners saved by grace. It is necessary for us to say this everywhere to everyone. I do not do this for your sake, but for my own, for this is my calling and I am compelled. At San Antonio when to my surprise The American Lutheran Church chose me among many able and fine men to carry this burden, I could only respond spontaneously and from deep within. For me the most beautiful confession of faith is that which I learned as a child in that country church from Luther's catechism: I believe that Jesus Christ, true God, begotten of the Father from all eternity, and also true man, born of the virgin Mary, is my Lord, who has redeemed me, a lost and condemned creature, bought and freed me from sin, death, and the power of the devil, not with silver or gold but with his holy and precious blood and his innocent sufferings and death, in order that I might be his own, live under him in his kingdom, and serve him in everlasting righteousness, innocence and blessedness, even as he lives and reigns to all eternity. This is most certainly true. And I believe that I cannot with my own reason or strength believe in Jesus Christ my Lord or come to him, but the

Holy Ghost has called me by the gospel, enlightened me with his gifts, and sanctified and preserved me in the true faith, just as he calls, gathers, enlightens and sanctifies the whole Christian church on earth and preserves it in union with Jesus Christ in the one true faith. This is the faith in which I live and for which I would die. And so would you.

Missouri Synod, we love you. We love you with the love of Christ, a love which is not of our making, but a gift from him. We pray for you, that you may do God's bidding, that your strength may be renewed like the eagle's that the Lord Jesus Christ may reign in your lives so that you may be his witnesses to the uttermost parts of the earth. You are God's people, Paul writes in Colossians. You are the people of God. He loved you and chose you for his own. Therefore, you must put on compassion, kindness, humility, gentleness and patience. Be helpful to one another and forgive one another, whenever any of you has a complaint against someone else. You must forgive each other in the same way that the Lord has forgiven you. And to all these add love, which binds all things together in perfect unity. The peace that Christ gives is to be the judge in your hearts, for to this peace God has called you together in the one body. How great is his grace! May God bless and keep you.

At the Memorial Service for William Larsen, 1971

Beloved in Christ Jesus. Death has many faces. As a fleeting image it conveys comfort, for it is a release from pain and sometimes from loneliness and despair. Johan Bach has captured this feeling for us in his pastoral "Come Sweet Death." Sometimes this impression grows stronger as a symbol of courage, as a sacrifice for a great cause. In secular history it is Socrates who stands as that symbol, and in our faith, our Lord as he sets his face toward Jerusalem.

But at its root, behind the masks, death is an enemy. It is a product of evil and of sin. It is our last enemy, in the words of St. Paul. It is not to be accepted as much as it is to be overcome. I cannot reconcile myself to the death of my friend Bill Larsen, at this stage of his life and from this cause. As Jesus wept for his friend Lazarus so I weep for my friend. And I weep for his wife and his children who must suffer this sting more than any of us who mourn with them. And I am angry that sin and death stalk man. A righteous anger, I pray, that will not be quiet when men suffer and die. I am comforted only with the knowledge that God is angry too! So angry that he submitted himself to the same suffering and death and overcame this enemy with his power and gives to us the fruits of his victory. He has invited us to share in his death and resurrection. And by his grace we accept and glory in this victory, and this is what gives us strength so that we are not crushed in our spirits, so that we can lift our heads high with hope and live for life knowing that we are more than conquerors.

In one of the little devotions that I had with Bill in the hospital we read from Colossians 1 and in this we rejoice that Jesus is Lord and he is to be in all things alone supreme.

The American Lutheran Church and its predecessor the United Evangelical Lutheran Church is thankful for the life and the service of this servant William Larsen. He had a remarkable career. A pastor, a chaplain to the armed forces, a chaplain to university students, a church president, a church vice-president, a church secretary, a leader and advisor to the great vocation of theological education, involved in international and national expressions of the Lutheran family. I believe that it was in his last calling he was most happy and gave his best. Always a student in theology, always open and growing in his involvement with people and social causes, he was for me and for many, many others a stalwart friend and a leader. We thank his wife and his family for having shared so much of him with us for so long. And we pray that the comfort and joy of God's victory will sustain them in the little time left for us all.

A Dream of God

SERMON AT PACIFIC LUTHERAN UNIVERSITY STUDENT CONGREGATION
October 31, 1971

Our Father in heaven, make us free men in Christ Jesus. Amen.

My colleagues in the faith, grace to you and peace from God our Father and the Lord Jesus Christ. Amen.

The text for the sermon this afternoon at the Reformation service will be the gospel, John 8. The text for our meditation here now will be the Old Testament lesson in Genesis 28, which was read to you.

Jacob dreamed a dream. In the chillness and the darkness of the Arabian desert, where the night is black and the stars are like diamonds, Jacob slept on a stone and dreamed of God. And that dream shaped Jacob and catapulted an obscure nomad in history as one of the founders of a great people which exists to this day as a stubborn, a tenacious, and a cohesive community. Jacob's dream was about the promise "Be sure that I will always be with you."

St. Paul dreamed a dream. A man stood on a distant shore and said, "Come over to Macedonia and help us." He followed his dream, and that was the beginning of the Christian era of the West.

Martin Luther dreamed a dream. Sitting in anguish in his tower, he gained an insight so deep and penetrating that it cut across all that he had learned and so molded him that he received both the intellectual power and the personal stamina to reform the church, a reformation which continues to this day in both intensity and in promise. Luther's dream was that the gospel had made him free.

Martin Luther King dreamed a dream. In the midst of the tensions and the hostilities, the blood and the sweat and the tears of this generation, he dreamed of a brotherhood of men for our society. And his dream still reverberates among us.

I wish for you a dream. My hope is that your life might have such a great cause, such a high ideal, such a penetrating understanding that everything you do and think is shaped by it. I covet for you fire in your soul, a fire which gives you direction and purpose, firmness and energy, so that your life is stirred, fed, and undergirded by it. Every person needs a dream. The irritations of life, the doubts at the edges, the obstacles and the uncertainties need to be subsumed under an overwhelming vision that life has a great counterweight which gives steadiness, persistence, and defines the goal. Life needs to be tied together so that efforts expended in work and in play contribute to a core of meaning worth a person's life.

I call you to a dream of God, an involvement, an excitement, an interest, a curiosity which will shape your energy and determine your destiny, a vision of God which has been embodied in the life of Jesus of Nazareth. Let him become the clue, the focal point, the model, and one can so easily love him.

I have a dream for PLU. My hope is it will build on the work of the forefathers, those who cut the stones and made the bricks and hewed the wood to make this university, and those who built here a monument, a pillar to the glory of God and to the task of proclaiming him. I dream of a PLU that will be remembered by you as the place of expanding understanding, of ever-deepening faith, of experiences of love, of the harboring of hope which will last for you a lifetime.

You are not so different from a Jacob or a Paul or a Luther or a

King, for you are persons. PLU is not so different from an Arabian desert, for the needs of human existence have followed every man through all of history. We share in common with all the past and even with future men the need for a dream and the possibility of one. The promise is the same for every human being: "Be sure that I will be with you." And Jacob built a monument, he built a pillar, and this pillar marked the place where he had met God. For a dream is not enough. Insights which are not concretized in the dimensions of character and in action slip away into a night of forgetfulness.

So I ask you also to build a pillar to mark your dream. And the avenues are many. You may build a pillar by expressing in your life with others the love which your dream has revealed as the goal and the ideal of life. You can build this pillar every day, wherever you are and whatever you do. Your thoughts, your words, your special efforts are the stones in the making of this kind of tower, a tower which can lift you high into the rare air of the discovery of the secret power in your life. You can build a pillar by the development of your character, by the control of your weaknesses, the weaknesses which you share with every other person, and the expansion of your strength. You can bring to expression your dream by prayer and communal worship, by involvement in the sacrificial giving of yourself to the needs of other persons. You have an advantage over Jacob, for your life is in the era of the resurrection and you have Jesus Christ as your model, and the shape of your deeds is there designed for following.

In your days in this place you have a great opportunity, for these years you are released from some, although not all, of the cares of life. This is the time and this is the place to dream and to build pillars. This is the place to make a Bethel, not because PLU is PLU but because this is where you are at this moment. Surely God is in this place, and he invites discovery.

And Jacob vowed a vow, as did Paul, and Luther, and King. Even dreaming and careful building are not enough. The stuff of life is also shaped by high resolve. The particular commitments and decisions of the great opportune moments harness the dreams and the character so that they can be handled and so they will prosper.

So I invite you to declare to yourself that these years will be the most important of your life thus far. Vow to discipline yourself commensurate with the task, to open yourself to change and to growth, to unleash the capacity which is within you to live beyond your performance in the past, to lift your eyes beyond the provinciality of the present moment to greater heights. Vow to set aside the grudges and the hostilities of the past, to being anew, separated from the problems, the failures, the false starts of the past to greet this new day with eagerness and with the wonderment of a Jacob alone in the night on the desert with the searing experience of a Luther high in an ancient tower. Vow to let nothing dissuade you from this dream, no professor in his slowness to understand you, no irritation from an artificial requirement or a troublesome disappointment, not even lack of confidence in yourself, nor even the pain of the failure to carry out the vow of a yesterday. For you know, you know, that there is forgiveness for your failure, power for your duties, learning from pain, opportunity in a changed view, comfort in God's acceptance even in your moments of despair. For the promise holds good. The opportunities which grow out of it are unfulfilled as yet for all of us.

It is in this spirit of Jacob and Paul and Luther and King that I invite you to celebrate the Reformation and to celebrate the memorial we call the Lord's Supper. Our dream is not only that he is present with us always but that in this special gift in the eucharist he focuses his love and his presence so that we are assured again, we are bound together and our hope is renewed. When you rise this day from this altar you are a new person. The old can be put away, the past is no more and you leave with all of life spread before you as a great new horizon. We shall come again to this experience, and we can walk in confidence because we know that we can come again. His promise holds good. He will always be here. How awe-inspiring is this place, for this is none other but the house of God, and this is the gate of heaven.

You are, of course, not a Jacob or a Paul or a Luther or a King because you are you, and you are just as important. But you may, in fact, you must, dream dreams, build your pillars, and make your vows, for you like every other man, are a child of this God, the God of Jacob and the Father of our Lord Jesus Christ. Amen.

The peace of God which passes all understanding keep your hearts and your minds through Christ Jesus. Amen.

The Terror of Victory

Sermon at the Southern District Convention
April 15, 1972

Dearly beloved, grace to you and peace from God our Father and the Lord Jesus Christ. Amen.

Our theme is *the terror of victory,* and our text is from the second chapter of Philippians, the great hymn to our Lord Jesus Christ. "Have this mind among yourselves, which you have in Christ Jesus, who though he was in the form of God did not count equality with God a thing to be grasped, but emptied himself, taking the form of a servant, being born in the likeness of men. And being found in human form he humbled himself, and became obedient unto death, even death on a cross. Therefore God has highly exalted him and bestowed on him the name which is above every name, that at the name of Jesus every knee should bow in heaven and on earth and under the earth, and every tongue confess that Jesus Christ is Lord, to the glory of God the Father."

It is a strange thing to call the cross a victory. It was a gory event. The blood and the water oozed from his body. There was the wrenching cry of thirst. There was the despair of abandonment, the stealth of the wicked, and there was a traitor. But it was a victory, despite its form and its image. This is precisely what it was and what it is.

The New Testament is a story about a war. It is a drama enacted against the backdrop of the glare of rockets and the mire of foxholes. There is brought into play the very foundations, not only of creation, but of God himself. For the cross was the climax of the fight to the death of God, the creator of all things, and his challenger. The stake in the awful game was man.

Given freedom by his creator, man chose to go his own way and enslaved himself to God's enemy. God in his grace and mercy chose to seek to break the grip of evil upon man and to restore him to his own kingdom, to bring him back to the destiny for which he had been created. Jesus, God's own Son and man's representative, was to bear the burden of the battle, to be both the victor and the victim in the great game to defeat the evil one and give man back his freedom. From Bethlehem to Golgotha the battle had raged, but at the end of the road on a lonely hill the climax came and the Redeemer announces his victory. "The strife was o'er, the battle done. Now is the victor's triumph won. Now be the song of praise begun. The powers of death have done their worst, but Christ their legions hath dispersed. Let shouts of holy joy outburst. Alleluia!" This is the language of the New Testament. A grand, exalted, sweeping language, breathtaking in its implications, unbelievable and yet haunting in its power to persuade and its capacity to inspire joy. This is our faith.

For us there is terror in this victory. To that lonely one who gave up all and endured the cross God has given the name the Lord. It is in the New Testament the highest name he can be given, for Paul says in Colossians he is the one who is in all things supreme. He is to be in all things supreme. And the terror is this, he cannot be escaped. He does not lie safely in that grave of long ago. This remembrance is not confined to an act in history relegated to books. History will not go back. He is Lord and before him all knees must bow. And the terror of decision for or against him is a direct consequence of his victory. A dead Lord is no problem. A living Lord requires attention.

Your relationship to him may be varied. You may ignore him. You may speak his words, his name upon your lips, but you may ignore him in what you do each day and what you think and feel deep within you, for you may be run by all kinds of forces, by economic forces—your real interest, that which grasps you and runs you, may be the gathering of things to you. It may be the power you have over other men. It may be self-aggrandizement which you consciously or unconsciously fare for yourselves. You can ignore him but you cannot escape him.

You may disobey him. You may know what he asks, you may know in certainty what he wants, but you choose to disobey him. But you cannot escape him. You may fight against him. You may say, this demand I will not do, this is unfair, this does not belong to this age, this is not a part of the reality of God, this is another cultural aberration. You can fight him and every man to a certain degree fights him and fights God. It is a part of your existence—there is given within you a desire to fight him. And in some ways there is something good about that, for if you fight him, then you recognize him. Then you know his demand and you are reacting to it, and in your battle with him there may emerge that obedience that he wants. You may fight him, but you cannot escape him.

You can ignore and escape your fellow men. You can destroy and escape your fellow men. You can fight and escape your fellow men, but you cannot escape a living Lord. And there lies the terror.

There is terror too because we are called to be like him. We are to have his mind. This means that we are to face the world in which we have been placed without grasping for the straws of a better or different world. We are to be like him in the place where we are, and not in a place where we would hope to be. The battle, you see, still rages. Its outcome is assured, the armistice has already been signed, but the enemy has not yet capitulated. The battle is now ours. To have his mind, to be his disciples, is to face the world as it is. The injustices in our society, the envy and the malice within ourselves, the demonic elements which sweep not only nations but whole civilizations, must be faced whatever the cost. He became obedient unto death. And this is our calling too.

Our calling is not to accommodate ourselves to the least line of resistance, but to hone the razor's edge of right and wrong. Our calling is not to retire into the comfort of a passive life, but to lead the vanguard for the gospel. Our calling is not to find fault with one another and to believe that all of life is dependent upon the shape and character of the response to our love. But our calling is to forgive. Our calling is not to hold onto that which we have managed for ourselves so that we become lords of that which is ours and guard it and guard it with all that is within us, but our calling is to expend ourselves. We do not have the gospel in our pockets. It is not ours to do with as we please. It is his gospel, and we are called upon to obey.

But the terror does not end even there. The terrors of decision and obedience are compounded by the terror of the future. The future is open. God promises nothing but ultimate victory. He does not promise a sure onward and upward path. God does not live by the rubrics of American economics. Growth is not necessarily in and of itself his promise. There is no resting place called Utopia upon the way. You and I may be the martyrs of these thousand years. There is no absolute gift from God except that of salvation. No promise sure of his in this world except that of the promise of the next. This is the style of life to which we have been called. It is a life which is shaped by hope and by courage. Courage, he cried, courage! There may be trouble in the world, but I have overcome the world. God called him Lord because he was obedient and overcame. We too will overcome when armed with his presence we trust and we work.

I ask of you some simple things. I ask you first of all to be an evangelist. For this is the essence, the shape, the nature of your discipleship. You are all evangelists. Not evangelists of the same kind, not following a particular technique. You are not all lay preachers, nor should you be, nor can you be. For to be an evangelist is not necessarily to be a preacher. An evangelist is to be one who lives by and for the gospel. Wherever you are and whatever you do, be motivated by, be shaped by, be thrust by, live by word and deed this freedom.

I ask you to be self-critical. Not self-critical in the sense of a deep foreboding and pessimism, of those entrepreneurs which find nothing of value in the world about them. But be self-critical in the New Testament sense of self-examination and repentance. For you have not yet learned everything. you are still pilgrims along the way, and you must be open to change. You must be willing to see that others have something to say, and the witness of other evangelists may be God's way of speaking to you. Be self-critical, and that means to be open and be bold.

Be bold. Not bold in a sense of arrogance, not bold in a sense of crashing through the sensitivities and feelings of others, but be bold in the sense that you have a goal and you have a method. You have a strategy for that goal and you pursue it. You are like the general of an army who makes his plans for battle. Sometimes to be bold means to keep one's mouth shut. Sometimes to be bold means to be patient. Sometimes to be bold means to give way. It takes courage sometimes to give way. But have your plan and be bold.

And lastly I ask you to be free. For this is the gift of the victory, is your liberation, is your freedom. Let me please, forgive me for a moment, if I tell you a little personal story that perhaps one or two of you may have heard. On the Saturday before Easter my daughter and son and wife and I got up very early in the morning and went to see my mother. She is 82. She has been ill from time to time, and we thought surely several weeks ago that she would die. And for this she is quite ready. It really in the end makes little difference to her whether she lives or dies. We went to see her then and we made our farewells. But this day when we arrived she was sitting in her chair with her best red dress, and she had fixed her hair, and she greeted us with a smile, and it was a happy day. In the afternoon my sister came in to say that her grandson and my mother's only great-grandchild had just been diagnosed as being a spastic, and you know what that means for the child and for the parents in the many years that lie ahead. We came back late that night, tired after an emotional day. But we got up early on Easter Sunday and went to sunrise service and a couple other services and rejoiced in one of those perfect days of togetherness and joy in resurrection and again went to bed late that night, as families are wont to do on those great days. And before we went to bed, my wife said to my daughter, "Let me take you back to college in the morning. You are very tired and the bus is not very comfortable. Let me run you down, and we'll take a couple of your friends." And she thought about it, but then my daughter said, "But mother, do you really want to go?" And she says, "No, I don't really want to go. It's a long ways, and you know I don't like to drive alone, and it may be slippery on the road." So it was decided that she would after all take the bus, and so we got up early the next morning, three mornings at 5:30 in a row, and we were tired, and we took her to the bus, and I placed her on it, and then I went to the office. At 1:00 the call came. The bus had overturned and there were injuries and several were killed. The first news broadcast that came out had said that our daughter had been killed. But she got to a pay phone in the hospital and called us and told us that she was all right. Each moment is given to us is a gift. We live, each one of us, by his grace. Nothing that is ours keeps us as we are, neither our will nor our possessions nor our intelligence nor our tenacity, nor our stubbornness nor our wisdom. Every moment to us is a gift. We live by his grace. And that is why we are free. Whether you are 82 or four months or 18 years, you are free because God has given you what you have and are. What are you holding on to? Why are you so afraid? Why is it you feel that somehow you must guide all these things? Be free. Be liberated in the gospel. Live in the joy of this victory. Garner this hope and face the future with courage. And work. Have his mind.

This morning we shall celebrate this victory, for that is the Lord's Supper. That marriage feast of the Lamb which is not yet, which lies there in the future we participate in today. In this very moment God comes into this place and gives us his Son's body and blood, and we celebrate that victory. This is the marriage feast of the Lamb in this moment. And in the strange world of God's time it is also that marriage feast of the future time and all time is exploded in this moment. We are no longer living only in a present moment, but we live in the past where his victory is brought, and we live in the future, where the future is brought into this moment. And this is no longer time, but this is the celebration of the presence of God, and we participate in it, and we too become victors. May God bless your communion.

What Evangelism Is

From the Address to the Minneapolis Convention, October 8, 1972

I solemnly call upon you in the presence of God and of Christ Jesus who will judge all men, living and dead, because of his coming and of his kingdom I command you to preach the message, to insist upon telling it whether the time is right or not, to convince, reproach and encourage teaching with all patience. Do the work of an evangelist and perform your whole duty as a servant of God. Our Father, we hear this solemn charge. We seek to obey this command. Enable us with the courage and wisdom of grace so that our lives will be shaped to live the gospel in word and deed. Amen.

Who is Christ Jesus? He is Lord. He is Lord. He is the one who stands over all the universe, who has won his place by his perfect obedience to the Father, the fighter who has conquered evil and has been made supreme over all.

Who is Jesus Christ? He is a Savior. He is the one who takes upon himself the hurts and the guilt and the hopes of all men, and he forgives. He forgives. If you would proclaim him, you must also be his disciple and you must follow him and he ministers to the pain, the guilt and the despair of all men and you too must forgive because he forgives you. And that's worth a very soft, praise the Lord.

Who is Jesus Christ? He is your friend. What a friend we have in Jesus. . . . He is the one who came to be with us, to know us, who identifies with us, who struggles with us, and who says, "I love you, I love you." He celebrates your humanity. He makes you a human being because he has come and stood beside you and made himself as you, and being you he celebrated his humanity and won, and becomes the perfect man in love toward the Father and perfect in his love for you. How can you say anything else but, I love you. If you proclaim Jesus Christ, you proclaim his love and his love is for every man. There is no distinction, there is no choice, if you love Jesus Christ then you love every man. There is no greater way to make your life of greater value than to know what Jesus Christ has done, to hear of his love and to say to him, "I love you." And that is praise the Lord.

If evangelism is something that comes from the word gospel, then it must involve fighting evil, it must mean ministering to the hurts and pains of all men, and it is driven by the love that demands to be shared without distinction. The proclamation of the grace of God manifested in Christ Jesus. But, what is grace? What is grace? Amazing grace, ah yes, but what is it? Grace, that is the only way that Jesus can be fully understood, and it is as the church in her long history and tradition, that is the word, that is the article by which the church stands or falls. What is grace? All that Jesus Christ means is that all he has done for me is freely given without any price. His victories are mine, his forgivenesses are mine, his love is pure, unadulterated, perfect, is mine. Grace is unconditioned, unlimited, a sheer gift. All that Jesus Christ has done and what he is, has been given freely to me.

Evangelism is the process of making alive that grace of the gospel. And that means that everyone who has heard of that grace, everyone who has been given that grace is an evangelist, and that means that it is everybody's business in the church. Evangelism is the soul of the church, is the life of the church—that doesn't mean worship isn't, or teaching isn't, it means that evangelism is the prior understanding of the character of the gospel. Evangelism is the coming alive of the gospel that requires teaching, requires worship and all of the many activities that we do—we do 435 activities in The American Lutheran Church. Did you know that? Evangelism is making the gospel alive in word and deed.

I've heard it said that evangelism and social action do not go together. I'm genuinely puzzled. If involvement is helping to right the wrongs of society and if that involvement is not motivated by the love of Jesus, then of course it is not the work of a Christian community. If evangelism is motivated by an attitude which refuses to show love to all persons, it is a distorted evangelism and may not be evangelism at all. When they brought a man sick of palsy to Jesus they started a conversation which finally led Jesus to say, "Which is it easier to say—your sins are forgiven" or "Take up your bed and walk?"

Evangelism is the communication of the whole gospel. Grace to man is spoken to the whole man. It is a manifestation of the grace which is in Christ Jesus to show love both to the body and to the soul, for the body and the soul are simply different ways to speak of the same whole person. Irradication of racism is the work of evangelism, the work of the gospel. The irradication of poverty is the work of the love of Jesus, and that is the work of the gospel, of evangelism. Whatever you do in the name of Jesus is a proclamation of the grace manifested in Christ Jesus. The irradication of the devastation of war is the work of evangelism, is the work of the gospel. If you treat every human being in a human way, if you can make a person whole in his spirit, give him hope, train him to become proud of his identity, help him to care for himself and his work, whatever you do to make the gospel alive, you proclaim the grace of God manifested in Christ Jesus.

Evangelism is the proclamation of the grace of God manifested in Jesus Christ. It is the thrusting forth of the gospel. Evangelism is everybody's business. No Christian is excused. Evangelism is making the gospel alive in both word and deed. Evangelism is obedience to the whole gospel. Evangelism is performing your whole duty as a servant of God.

As the servant of God, rejoice in the gospel. Celebrate this free given grace which is given to you and let that grace thrust forth and overflow so your whole life sparkles and you hold back nothing to any man, to any man. Be to every man Jesus Christ—obey him—obey him, and then you may hope, then you may celebrate and then your destiny comes alive, for Jesus Christ is your Lord, your Savior and your friend.

Bibliography of Kent S. Knutson Material

1. 1950, Oct.
   Foreword to study booklet "Thy Word Is Truth," LSAA. 1 p., xerox
   The Word of God
2. 1950, Oct.
   "From Our President," *Campus Lutheran* (LSAA magazine), p. 2. 1 p., xerox
   This column was written monthly while he was president of the LSAA. This article's theme is that God uses the LSAA.
3. 1950, Nov.
   "From Our President," *Campus Lutheran,* p. 2. 1 p., xerox
   Call to commitment.
4. 1951, Jan.
   "From Our President," *Campus Lutheran,* p. 2. 1 p., xerox
   Love and hope of Christ in a chaotic world.
5. 1951, Feb.
   "From Our President," *Campus Lutheran,* p. 2. 1 p., xerox
   Prayer in Lent.
6. 1951, Mar.
   "From Our President," *Campus Lutheran,* p. 2. 1 p., xerox
   Lutheran heritage and beliefs.

7. 1951, Apr.
"From Our President," *Campus Lutheran*, p. 2. Reprinted in *Lutheran Student Movement Newsletter*, March, 1974.
1 p., xerox

The Christian in society.

8. 1951, May
"From Our President," *Campus Lutheran*, p. 2. 1 p., xerox
1951 Ashram

9. 1951, Summer
"From Our President," *Campus Lutheran*, p. 2. 1 p., xerox
1951 Ashram

10. 1951, Aug.
Report of the President to the Lutheran Student Council of America, Interlochen, Michigan. 8 pp., xerox

11. 1952, Nov.
"Dream or Reality?" *Campus Lutheran*, pp. 4-9. 3 pp., xerox
The Lutheran Student Movement.

12. 1952, Dec.
Christmas letter 2 pp., printed

13. 1953, Nov.
"Can Science Discover God?" *Campus Lutheran*, pp. 2-4ff.
4 pp., xerox

Truth as object of our search, as God's gift that possesses us; universality as seeker after truth, church as bearer of truth.

14. 1954
"Concerning Semantics," LSA Program Series, 1954, reprinted in WITNESS, a manual on campus evangelism, 1955.
4 pp., xerox

Definitions of theological and philosophical words.

15. 1954, May 30
Service of ordination 4 pp., xerox

16. 1956, Apr.
"In Review . . . ", *Frontiers* (LSAA Magazine), pp. 29-30.
2 pp., xerox

Review of *The Protestant Tradition* by J. S. Whale and *The Strangeness of the Church* by Daniel Jenkins.

17. 1961

The Community of Faith and the Word: An Inquiry into the Concept of the Church in Contemporary Lutheranism. Doctoral thesis, Columbia University, Union Theological Seminary, 1961. Published by University Microfilms. Available in the library. 372 pp.

18. 1961, June 11

Sermon at the ordination of Sigurd Arneson. 1 cassette (NT)

Task of a minister: to interpret the Lordship of Christ by probing the mind of modern man and preaching modern Christ to him.

19. 1962

"The Unshrunk Cloth," paper given at ALC Stewardship Conference. 6 pp., mimeo

The world to whom we proclaim the gospel has changed: (1) it does not believe in the God of the Bible; (2) it no longer understands covenant community; (3) its picture of the world is bigger than its picture of God.

20. 1962

"New Wine," paper given at ALC Stewardship Conference. 4 pp., mimeo

Preaching the entire gospel to a changed world: we need to stress "theology of response" (God acts in our lives continually), "theology of community" (Christians as ministers of reconciliation), "theology of success" (or responsibility), "theology of nature."

21. 1962, Winter

"Pluralism in Lutheran Ecclesiology," *Dialog,* pp. 59-66. (See also 1965, God's People Living in Fellowship, Part II, B.) 8 pp., xerox

Four Lutheran interpretations of the church and implications thereof: (1) Repristination theology (Pieper), (2) pietism (Hallesby), (3) Lundensian (Aulen and Nygren), (4) Neo-Confessionalism (Schlink, *et al.*)

22. 1962, Feb. 5-6

The Doctrine of the church and its implications for parish education, paper. 6 pp., mimeo

Defines the church as both human and divine, as where

the gospel is, in terms of relationship of faith and grace. Draws implications for teaching: it is the church's work, it is to fulfill faith. Explicates teaching in terms of the one, holy, catholic, apostolic church. Baptism as the context of teaching.

23. 1962, Autumn
"Christian and Citizen An Answer," *Dialog,* pp. 58-60.
3 pp., xerox
Answer to an attack by Victor R. Gold of a statement released by Knutson and others supporting JFK before the 1960 election. (The Gold article is also on p. 58.)

24. 1963
Patterns of Community in Lutheran Ecclesiology, paper. This is "Community and the Church" article in *The New Community in Christ,* ed. by James H. Burtness and John P. Kildahl, Augsburg, 1963. 28 pp., mimeo
The doctrine of the church in Luther and Knutson's four patterns in contemporary Lutheran theology (see 1962, Winter—"Pluralism . . .")

25. 1963
The Christian Community and the Citizen Community, paper. This is "Christian Community and Citizen Community," article in *The Silent Struggle for Mid-America,* ed. by Elwin W. Mueller, Augsburg, 1963. 14 pp., mimeo
The relationship of the church in which a Christian lives to the society in which he lives. The responsibilities of the Christian and the church in society.

26. 1963, Feb. 20
"The 'One Seminary' Concept," paper. 8 pp., xerox
The ALC seminaries should cooperate in their one goal but not be required to be in complete uniformity.

27. 1963, Aug. 27
"Dimensions of a Dialog; Personal Reactions to Montreal," *Lutheran Standard,* pp. 12-13ff. 3 pp., xerox

28. 1964
"Some Terms Related to Our Understanding of God's Word," a lecture given at a pastoral retreat of Southern Wisconsin pastors at Green Lake, Wisconsin. 10 pp., xerox

29. 1964, Winter
"New Wine for Fresh Skins," *Dialog,* pp. 42-47. (See 1962—Unshrunk Cloth and New Wine.) 6 pp., xerox
To a changed world (describes how it has changed) we must preach the whole gospel of Jesus Christ (describes what we have been missing).

30. 1964, Jan. 14
"Exactly What IS the Church?" *Lutheran Standard,* pp. 12ff. 3 pp., xerox
Commonly held pictures of the church which are not true to our doctrine of the church.

31. 1964, Jan. 28
"Images of the Church," *Lutheran Standard,* pp. 4-6. (Cont. from January 14) 3 pp., xerox
Church as the called-out people, the body of Christ, the foretaste of the kingdom of God.

32. 1964, May 9
Letter to Dr. Schiotz. 4 pp., xerox
Outline of his convictions about Lutheran unity. He argues for a declaration of fellowship with LCA now.

33. 1964, Summer
"Ecumenical Perspectives: Article VII and the Fellowship Question among Lutherans," *Dialog,* pp. 223-225. 3 pp., xerox
The problem of altar and pulpit fellowship among American Lutherans: The ALC must take the initiative.

34. 1964, July 8
"Biblical Ethics in an Altered Society," lecture at The Lutheran Free Conference in Great Britain, a conference of Lutheran pastors sponsored by The Lutheran Free Conference in cooperation with the Lutheran World Federation Department of Theology, at Mansfield College, Oxford, July 7-10, 1964. 9 pp., mimeo

35. 1965
The Lord's Supper: The Gospel in Action, paper. 9 pp., mimeo
The Lord's Supper: in biblical research, theologically, what the churches are doing about it, and a theology for Lutherans.

36. 1965
"The Community of the Church," four contemporary Lutheran interpretations of the community of the church. Outline. (See 1962, Winter—"Pluralism . . .") 2 pp., mimeo

37. 1965, May
God's People Living in Fellowship, resource and material for ALC Theme for 1967. 179 pp., mimeo
Part I: A history of fellowship as unity (or disunity) in the church from New Testament to the present (pp. 1-50)
Part II: The church in the Augsburg Confession, and four views of the church in contemporary Lutheranism (see 1962, Winter—"Pluralism . . .") (pp. 51-101)
Part III: Word Studies (pp. 102-122)
Part IV: Fellowship as part of the nature of the church, especially in the sacraments (pp. 123-161)
Part V: Bibliography (pp. 162-179)

38. 1965, Oct. 6
"Baptism and Christian Education," statement at Board of Parish Education meeting. 19 pp., mimeo
How to deal with baptism in writing a curriculum, and some of the attitudes in the church that present a problem.

39. 1966, Winter
"Dialog—The Fifth Year," an editorial, *Dialog,* pp. 4-6. 3 pp., xerox
A critique.

40. 1966, Jan. 11
"Always on the Way," *Lutheran Standard,* pp. 6-7.
Uses key words to describe the theological outlook of the ALC.
2 pp., xerox

41. 1966, Apr. 15
"Some Guidelines as to the Lutheran View of the Church in the World." Thesis statements. 2 pp., mimeo

42. 1966, Fall
"Theological Issues in the Ecumenical Movement: Survey of Attitudes." 2 pp., mimeo

43. 1966, Sept. 23-25
"Contemporary Lutheran Theology and the Eucharistic Sacri-

fice," paper. 17 pp., mimeo
Lutherans must re-evaluate their thinking about Eucharistic sacrifice in order to find a basis for discussion with Roman Catholics.

44. 1966-67?
Human Potentiality and the Teaching Ministry of the Church, paper. 22 pp., mimeo
Theology and teaching in the church.

45. 1967
How Shall We Speak of the Church? paper—manuscript with marginal notes. 13 pp., xerox
The church in the New Testament, signs of the church, the church and the Reformation, ministry

46. 1967
Foreword to *The Final Act* by Peter Kjeseth, as editor of the Tower Books series. 1 p., xerox

47. 1968
The Hope of the Life to Come, paper (See 1970—Kent Knutson on Resurrection.) 4 pp., mimeo
Why and how he believes in the resurrection.

48. 1968, Jan. 23
"Learning to Trust the Gospel," *Lutheran Standard,* pp. 5-7. 3 pp., xerox
Areas of growth and problems in the church at the 450th anniversary of the Reformation.

49. 1968, Feb. 21-22
Comments on "Preliminary Theses on the Ministry and Ordination." 3 pp., mimeo

50. 1968, June 17
"The Authority of the Scripture—An Evangelical Approach," speech given to the seventh annual Institute on Theology in Practice Today at Concordia Seminary, St. Louis. 17 pp., mimeo
Definition of Word of God as Bible, Gospel and ministry, and theses on what the authority of the Word means.

51. 1968, October
Address to the Omaha Convention on accepting the presidency

of Wartburg Seminary. 2 pp., mimeo
Challenge to discover what we are as the church.

52. 1968, Dec. 24
Christmas Eve sermon 1 cassette (NT)
Incarnation

53. 1969
1969 Parish Education Yearbook: Education and Confirmation, Chapter 3: "A Theological Point of View." 19 pp., mimeo
A new definition and new ways of confirmation are needed in the church.

54. 1969, Winter
"The Expanding Borders of Christian Fellowship," *The Lutheran Chaplain,* pp. 6-8. 3 pp., xerox
Ecumenism and its theological bases; Lutheran-Catholic dialogues; inter-Lutheran fellowship.

55. 1969, Feb.
"Musings on the Future of American Lutheranism," *Lutheran Quarterly,* pp. 44-52. 9 pp., xerox
Future of American Lutheranism must encompass a variety of opinions (but not rifts), cooperation among all Lutherans in both fellowship and structure, cooperation with other traditions, and learn to thrive in American culture and remain Lutheran.

56. 1969, Feb.
Ambassador interview of Dr. Knutson by Dave Holmquist and Larry Christensen. Published in May, 1969, *Ambassador.*
35 pp., typescript (from tape)
Ministry and ministers, seminary education, Wartburg, secular ministry, the role of the church.

57. 1969, Mar.
"The Authority of the Scripture," *Concordia Theological Monthly,* pp. 156-165. (See 1968, June 17, address.)
10 pp., xerox

58. 1969, May
"'S' Is for 'Sigvar'", an *Ambassador* interview with Dr. Kent S. Knutson, *Ambassador,* pp. 3-9. 4 pp., xerox

59. 1969, June

A Proposal for Cooperation in Graduate Education Among Minnesota Theological Seminaries. 63 pp., xerox

60. 1969, Summer
"To Cluster or Not?" an editorial, *Dialog,* p. 164. 1 p., xerox
Pros and Cons of inter-seminary cooperation.

61. 1969, Sept. 19
Inaugural address as President of Wartburg Seminary printed in the *Ambassador* as "The Celebration of a Task," November 1969.

62. 1969, Oct.
"On the Question of Rebaptism of Mormons When They Enter the Lutheran Church," statement. 2 pp., mimeo
Generally we ought to baptize Mormons.

63. 1969, Nov.
"The Celebration of a Task," *Ambassador,* pp. 12-23. Inaugural address of President of Wartburg Seminary, September 19, 1969. 6 pp., xerox
The theological task of interpreting the gospel to the church and the world and some implications of that.

64. 1969, Nov.
"The National Crisis Fund and Wartburg Seminary," *Ambassador,* pp. 4-6. 2 pp., xerox

65. 1970
Kent Knutson on resurrection. Lecture given at Free University, Wartburg Seminary. (See The Hope of the Life to Come, 1968.) 16 pp., typescript (from tape)

66. 1970, Mar. 3
"Revenge Is a Word We Know," *Lutheran Standard,* pp. 10-11. (Taken from *God's Drama in Seven Acts.*) 2 pp., xerox
Forgiveness is alien to us, but we receive God's forgiveness.

67. 1970, May
Letter to alumni of Wartburg Seminary. 1 cassette (NT)

68. 1970, May 12
"Theological Elephants," *Lutheran Standard,* pp. 10-11. 2 pp., xerox
Theological trends among students.

69. 1970, July 17
The Response of the Lutheran Churches to the Roman Catholic Church and Theology Today, public lecture, Fifth Assembly of the Lutheran World Federation, July 17, 1970, Evian, France. (See 1970, October—*Lutheran World.*) 16 pp., mimeo
Lutheran-Catholic relations since Vatican II and the need to continue and expand cooperation.
70. 1970, Sept. 15-16
Speech at 57th annual meeting of National Lutheran Editors and Managers Association, Minneapolis, printed in *The Lutheran Scholar,* January and April, 1971, "Theological Issues in the Lutheran Church in the 1970s."
71. 1970, Oct.
Tribute to Dr. Schiotz given at San Antonio convention print-in *Lutheran Standard,* Dec. 8, 1970, "Hero of the Unsung."
72. 1970, Oct.
"The Response of the Lutheran Churches to the Roman Catholic Church and Theology Today," *Lutheran World,* pp. 330-340. (See July 17, 1970 lecture.) 11 pp., xerox
73. 1970, Oct. 23
"To the Delegates of the American Lutheran Church Convention, 1970," a personal statement. 2 pp., mimeo
What our church needs in its president.
74. 1970, Oct. 23
Acceptance speech, delivered on Friday, October 23, 1970, after his election as President of the ALC, to the convention.
4 pp., typescript (from tape)
75. 1970, Nov.
"The Splendor of the Church," The *Ambassador,* pp. 2-3.
2 pp., xerox
Text of acceptance speech, October 23, 1970.
76. 1970, Dec. 8
"Hero of the Unsung," *Lutheran Standard,* pp. 2-4.
3 pp., xerox
Tribute to Dr. Schiotz given at San Antonio convention.
77. 1971?
"Contemporary Reality of the Church," side 2 of cassette on the Nature of the Church, from Luther Theological Seminary

Cassette Service. (See also "The Reformation and Modern Man," October 31, 1971.) (See also Chapter 6 of *The Shape of the Question.)*

Reformation theology is viable for the church today.

78. 1971

The State of the Church: Hope and Anxiety; Report of the President of the American Lutheran Church to the District Conventions, 1971. 8 pp., printed

Call for Lutheran unity, and the church as the people of God in a time of change.

79. 1971, Jan.

"Theological Issues in the Lutheran Church in the 1970s," *The Lutheran Scholar,* pp. 28-32. Concluded in the April issue. Article prepared from notes taken at the 57th annual meeting of National Lutheran Editors and Managers Association, Minneapolis, September 15-16, 1970. 3 pp., xerox

The theological questions of the Reformation are still valid: ways of looking at reality, faith, ethics, church forms.

80. 1971, Jan. 5

"But Some Things Don't Change," *Lutheran Standard,* pp. 2-5. 4 pp., xerox

The gospel is unchanging.

81. 1971, Feb. 2

"A Great Church," *Lutheran Standard,* p. 13. 1 p., xerox

Some of the things we need to do to do the work of the church.

82. 1971, March

"Dear Fellow Ministers," *Commentator,* pp. 4-7. printed

Commentator articles are reports and comments about the business of the church, comments about concerns of the president, and other necessary and helpful communications from the president to clergy and lay leaders of the ALC. This one is mainly about restructuring.

83. 1971, March

"The Doctrine of Scripture as Taught in the American Lutheran Church," a paper presented to Commission on Fellowship of The American Lutheran Church and the LC-MS in

March, 1971. This is a personal statement, not an official paper. Appended is a 2 page letter of criticism by Warren Quanbeck. 11 pp., mimeo

The significance of our commitment to the Scriptures and the Confessions. The doctrine of the Word and some words that are causing problems in the Lutheran Church today.

84. 1971, March 9?

"Doctrine of the Word and Fellowship for Lutherans Today," Speech to pastors of LCA, ALC, and LC-MS in Milwaukee. 1 cassette (NT)

The question of scripture as it is the basis for some problems in the Lutheran Church today and the question of ecumenical relations in the World Council of Churches and Lutheran World Federation.

85. 1971, Mar. 9

"State of the Lutheran Church Today," speech before the Lutheran Council of Metro-Milwaukee. 2 videotapes (NT)

Content unknown.

86. 1971, Mar. 27

Address to the Eastern North Dakota District Convention at Grand Forks, N.D. 8 pp., typescript (from tape)

1971 report to districts.

87. 1971, Apr.

"Theological Issues in the Lutheran Church in the 1970s," *Lutheran Scholar,* pp. 63-64. Continued from the January issue. 2 pp., xerox

88. 1971, Apr.

"Dear Fellow Ministers," *Commentator,* pp. 4-7. printed

Prayer for peace, stewardship, constitutional amendments, and anonymous letters.

89. 1971, Apr. 6

"What Is a Lutheran?" *Lutheran Standard,* p. 13. 1 p., xerox

Lutherans are bound by their confession of faith in the gospel.

90. 1971, May

"Dear Fellow Ministers," *Commentator,* pp. 6-7. printed

A number of various subjects.

91. 1971, May 4
"Speaking/Acting the Faith," *Lutheran Standard,* p. 16.
1 p., xerox
Speaking the gospel and acting responsibly toward the world.

92. 1971, May 11-14
Address at South Pacific District Convention.
22 pp., typescript (from tape)
1971 report to districts.

93. 1971, May 11-14
Lecture devotional at South Pacific District Convention. (See also June, 1972 address at ELCC Convention, and ch. 2 of *The Shape of the Question.)* 1 cassette (NT)
The power of God and the power he gives the church.

94. 1971, May 14
Address at Western North Dakota District Convention.
2 cassettes (NT)

95. 1971, May 30
"The Human Be-In," commencement address at St. Olaf.
7 pp., xerox

96. 1971, June
"Dear Fellow Ministers," *Commentator,* pp. 8-9. printed
Restructuring.

97. 1971, July 13
Address at LC-MS Convention in Milwaukee. This cassette is Vol. I, no. 8 of *Clergy,* August, 1971. 1 cassette (NT)
ALC-LCMS fellowship and problems seen by LCMS.

98. 1971, July 13
"Dr. Kent Knutson," excerpts from address to LCMS convention in August, 1971 issue of *Milwaukee Lutheran.*
1 p., xerox

99. 1971, July 18
Sermon at installation of Roy Gilbertson as Western North Dakota District President. 1 cassette (NT)
We celebrate the church—the chosen people of God and the body of Christ—and we celebrate God's grace and hope.

100. 1971, Aug. 8
Statement at the memorial service for William Larsen.
2 pp., xerox

101. 1971, Sept.
"Dear Fellow Ministers," *Commentator,* pp. 7-10. printed
A number of issues, including the LCMS convention.

102. 1971, Sept. 7
"Fellowship with other Lutherans," *Lutheran Standard,* p. 19.
1 p., xerox

103. 1971, Sept. 30
Notes on Address to the Boards related to Congregational Life.
2 pp., mimeo
Identity and mission of the ALC.

104. 1971, Oct.
Report of the President to the Church Council of The American Lutheran Church. (See also 1972 Report to the Districts.)
10 pp., mimeo
ALC internally and as it relates to the other churches.

105. 1971, Oct.
"Dear Fellow Ministers," *Commentator,* pp. 6-8. printed
How the ALC deals with the wage-price freeze, how to deal with the problem of moving personnel, and preaching.

106. 1971, Oct. 5
"Gospel and Reformation," *Lutheran Standard,* pp. 13-14.
2 pp., xerox
The gospel is universal, it frees us, it makes us human, it unites us, it impels us to love. We celebrate it at Reformation.

107. 1971, Oct. 25-27
Two lectures at South Pacific Pastor's Retreat in Palm Desert, California. 2 cassettes (NT)
(1) Classical Christology (see ch. 3 of *The Shape of the Question*).
(2) Doctrine of the Word and Contemporary Accents in Christology.

108. 1971, Oct. 28
"The Need for Planning and Systemization," a presentation

at a workshop on programmatic concerns for certain staff persons carrying programmatic responsibilities for the various boards of the American Lutheran Church.
10 pp., typescript transcribed from cassette

109. 1971, Oct. 31
Sermon at Pacific Lutheran University student congregation on the occasion of the installation of Pastor Gordon Lathrop as university minister at PLU. 1 cassette (NT)
Dream the dream that guides your life—like Jacob's dream.

110. 1971, Oct. 31
"The Reformation and Modern Man," speech given at PLU. Also a version entitled "The Reformation—A Fountainhead of the Modern World," 3 p. (See also Ch. 6 of *The Shape of the Question.)* 11 pp., manuscript and longhand notes
We are influenced by Reformation thinking.

111. 1971, Nov.
"Dear Fellow Ministers," *Commentator,* pp. 6-10. printed
The right to dissent, restructuring, and the WCC.

112. 1971, Nov. 2
"Lutherans and Other Christians," *Lutheran Standard,* pp. 15, 28. 2 pp., xerox
Ecumenical movement and World Council of Churches.

113. 1971, Nov. 14-16
The Minot Gullixson Memorial Lectures, First Lutheran Church, Minot, North Dakota. Four lectures. Eventuated in *The Shape of the Question.* four cassettes (NT)
(1) "The power of God" and the power he gives his church. (See ch. 2, and June 1972 ELCC convention.)
(2) "The Shape of the Question"—secularism. (See ch. 1)
(3) "The Christ of Tradition—The Method for Mission" and "Communicating Christ Today—A Method of Models." (See ch. 3 and 4.)
(4) "The Future of Lutheranism in America." (See Feb., 1969, "Musings . . .")

114. 1971, Dec.
"Dear Fellow Ministers," *Commentator,* pp. 4-6. printed
Report on the church council meeting, Oct. 18-22.

115. 1971, Dec. 21
"The God Who Comes at Christmas," *Lutheran Standard,* pp. 38-39. 2 pp., xerox
Incarnation.

116. 1972, I
"Relationship of Evangelism to the Faith and Mission of the Church," prepared by Commission on Evangelism to acquaint people of the church with Key 73. cassette (NT)
Evangelism is that which binds together what the church believes (faith) and what the church does (mission). It is living by the gospel. All of us are called to be evangelists.

117. 1972
Foreword to *Search for Understanding,* by Warren Quanbeck, Augsburg, 1972, pp. 7-8. 1 p., xerox
Short introduction on ecumenical movement.

118. 1972
Foreword to *Lutheranism in North America* by E. Clifford Nelson, Augsburg, 1972, pp. ix-xii. 3 pp., xerox
Essay on the Lutheran Church in America today as it is influenced by the debate about the authority of the scriptures, in its ministry to this society, among younger Lutherans, the gospel in the Lutheran church, and unity among Lutherans.

119. 1972
Report of the General President to the Church Council, 1972. 53 pp., mimeo
Brief comments on cooperation with LCA and LCMS, ALC restructuring, district constitution, and retirement of national staff. The rest of the report is "Implementation of the Proposal 'Toward Greater Effectiveness for Mission.'"

120. 1972, Jan.
The State of the Church, report of the President of the American Lutheran Church to the Districts. Revision of report to church council, 1971. 12 pp., printed

121. 1972, Jan.
"To My Fellow Ministers," *Commentator,* pp. 2-4. printed
How Phase II affects the ALC.

122. 1972, Jan. 4
"The Mission of the Church," *Lutheran Standard,* p. 13. 1 p., xerox
Expanding concept of mission.

123. 1972, Feb.
"To My Fellow Ministers," *Commentator,* pp. 2-4. printed

124. 1972, Feb. 3
Address at LECNA Convention—see Chapter 6 of *The Shape of the Question.* 14 pp., xerox

125. 1972, Feb. 15
"Resources for Mission," *Lutheran Standard,* p. 13. 1 p., xerox
Resources are the gospel, people, mission strategy and money.

126. 1972, March
"To My Fellow Ministers," *Commentator,* pp. 3-5. printed
Immortality, Vietnam war, and Phase II.

127. 1972, March 15
"Toward Greater Effectiveness for Mission," a proposal for new structures in the national offices of the American Lutheran Church. 43 pp., printed
History of restructuring attempts and assumptions made, outline of new structures, and Knutson's comments.

128. 1972, Mar. 21
"Easter Joy," *Lutheran Standard,* p. 13. 1 p., xerox
Easter as God's event for man's salvation and hope.

129. 1972, April
"To My Fellow Ministers," *Commentator,* pp. 3-6. printed
Various issues.

130. 1972, Apr. 4
"How Great His Grace," *Lutheran Standard,* pp. 12-13. From address to Milwaukee convention of LC-MS, July 13, 1971. 2 pp., xerox
ALC-LCMS fellowship.

131. 1972, April 7
"The Church, the College, and the Mission," speech given at a gathering of Lutheran college alumni at Augsburg College, Minneapolis. 9 pp., mimeo

The mission of the church college as a particular and necessary part of the mission of the church.

132. 1972, Apr. 15
Address to Southern District Convention. 1 cassette (NT)
Report to district.

133. 1972, Apr. 15
Sermon at Southern District Convention. 1 cassette (NT)
The Cross as victory, Jesus Christ is our living Lord. Be evangelist, self-critical, bold, and free.

134. 1972, April 18
"Strategy for Mission," *Lutheran Standard.* 1 p., xerox
Ways to carry out the mission of the church.

135. 1972, May
"To My Fellow Ministers," *Commentator,* pp. 3-5. printed
Restructuring and other issues.

136. 1972, May 7
"Celebrate Grace," sermon at St. Paul's, Waverly, Iowa.
8 pp., typescript (from tape)
The church's mission is to minister in the world in which it lives and to celebrate the gospel which makes us the church.

137. 1972, May 23
Address at North Pacific District Convention at PLU.
1 cassette (NT)
Report to district.

138. May 28
"The dilemmas which face man are not new. . . ." Sermon at Thiel College. 2 pp., manuscript with notes
You may be God's person for this time, like Esther.

139. 1972, June
"To My Fellow Ministers," *Commentator,* pp. 2-4. printed
Various issues.

140. 1972, June 19-23
Address delivered at the Evangelical Lutheran Church of Canada convention at Camrose, Alberta. (See Chap. 2 of *The Shape of the Question.)* 23 pp., typescript (from tape)
The power of God and the power he gives his church for mission.

141. 1972, June 19-23
Sermon preached at ELCC convention.
9 pp., typescript (from tape)
The gospel as perceived by faith, as gracious (that is, for me), revealed through the Word, and our response.
142. 1972, June 4
Address to South Dakota District Convention.
1 cassette (NT)
Report to district.
143. 1972, June 4
Sermon at South Dakota District Convention.
1 cassette (NT)
See also sermon at ELCC convention, June 19-23, 1972. The gospel as perceived by faith, for me, comes to me here in the world, and my response.
144. 1972, June 20
"Mission and Growth," *Lutheran Standard,* p. 13. 1 p., xerox
Implications for the church of the numerical decline in membership.
145. 1972, July 18
"You Are the Key," *Lutheran Standard,* p. 21. 1 p., xerox
Evangelism.
146. 1972, Aug. 15
"The Mission and Me," *Lutheran Standard,* p. 13. 1 p., xerox
Evangelism.
147. 1972, Sept.
"To My Fellow Ministers," *Commentator,* pp. 2-4. printed
Lutheran World Federation.
148. 1972, Sept. 19-20
Minutes of the ALC Stewardship Committee Meeting.
1 p., mimeo
Comments about churches visited on trip, about ALC and LCMS, gospel, social responsibilities, ALC budget.
149. 1972, Oct.
"Prospects for the LWF," *Lutheran World,* pp. 358-361.
4 pp., xerox
The significance of membership in the LWF for American Lutherans.

150. 1972, Oct.
"Is Fellowship Possible?" *Ecumenical Review,* pp. 459-470.
12 pp., xerox
Problems involved in fellowship among the churches of the WCC, and affirmations of fellowship. Discovering and defining what fellowship is.

151. 1972, Oct.
"To My Fellow Ministers," *Commentator,* pp. 2-3. printed
World missions.

152. 1972, Oct.
President's Report to the 1972 General Convention.
12 pp., xerox of manuscript with hand-written notes

153. 1972, Oct. 7
"Secularization Worries Lutheran Leader," by James M. Johnston, *Milwaukee Sentinel,* p. 22, part 1. 2 pp., xerox

154. 1972, Oct. 8
"Evangelism is a Gospel Word. . . ." Evangelism address at convention. 8 pp., typescript and longhand

155. 1972, Oct. 8
"I solemnly call upon you . . ." evangelism address at convention.
We have three copies of this speech, one from the tape, one from an abridged tape, and his own manuscript. We also have a tape of this speech.

156. 1972, Oct. 24
"The Mission and the World," *Lutheran Standard,* pp. 20-21.
2 pp., xerox
Churches he visited on his tour.

157. 1972, Nov.
"To My Fellow Ministers," *Commentator,* pp. 2-6. printed
World Council of Churches and other things.

158. 1972, Nov. 7
"Money—For the Real Things in Life," *Lutheran Standard,* p. 17. 1 p., xerox
Stewardship.

159. 1973, Mar. 15
Memorial service, Loehe Chapel, Wartburg. cassette

160. 1973, Apr. 3
Quotations on death from *His Only Son, Our Lord* and from his statement at the funeral of Dr. William Larsen, *Lutheran Standard,* p. 23. 1 p., xerox

161. Undated (1969-1970)
"The Church and Secularity," a critique of a paper by Father Masterson. 6 pp., mimeo
The church, the absurdity of the human condition, and hope in Christ.

162. Undated
The Constant and the Changing in Christian Mission, a paper. 20 pp., mimeo
A philosophical investigation of the question, what is the gospel and does it change.

163. Undated
The Doctrine of Man in the Lutheran Confessions, submitted for PR 265, The Christian View of Human Nature. 23 pp., mimeo

164. Undated
Four meditations for nursery roll mothers. 13 pp., mimeo

165. Undated
"On Having a Faith" 5 pp., manuscript with notes
Faith in Jesus Christ as the meaningful alternative to a meaningless and anxious life.